Family Secrets

Family Secrets

Derek Malcolm

W F HOWES LTD

This large print edition published in 2004 by
W F Howes Ltd
Units 6/7, Victoria Mills, Fowke Street
Rothley, Leicester LE7 7PJ

1 3 5 7 9 10 8 6 4 2

First published in 2003 by Hutchinson

A CIP catalogue record for this book is available
from the British Library

ISBN 1 84505 678 7

Typeset by Palimpsest Book Production Limited,
Polmont, Stirlingshire
Printed and bound in Great Britain
by Antony Rowe Ltd, Chippenham, Wilts.

For my father – by nurture
if not by nature

ACKNOWLEDGEMENTS

In telling this extraordinary story of a violent death that happened long before I was born but which had consequences that affected the lives of both my parents and myself over half a century later, I was well aware that some might think I should have remained silent. It concerned those I grew to love but not to blame. And I hope this book in no way sullies their memory.

I could not have written it without the total support of my wife, Sarah Gristwood, who did some valuable initial research despite being in the throes of a book of her own, or the encouragement and patience of David O'Leary, my agent, and Paul Sidey, my publisher. I would also like to thank the film-maker Jon Sanders who kept spurring me on and Daniel and Emily Kahn and the *Guardian*'s Archive department for their research on the court case. I never quite believed the old saw that the truth is often stranger than fiction until I discovered the intimate details behind this family secret. Now I most certainly do.

CONTENTS

Douglas Malcolm, soon after his marriage.

PROLOGUE

MY VERY OWN DARLING

Early on the morning of 14 August, 1917, Lieutenant J. Douglas Malcolm, home in London on leave from active duty on the Western Front, walked out of his Knightsbridge apartment, leaving a despairing letter for Dorothy, the wife he had married shortly before volunteering.

My very own darling Dorothy,

Dear God . . . this creature is the most insufferable blackguard that was ever born . . . that he ever dared even speak to you drives me mad. I simply can't stand it any longer. I am going to thrash him until he is unrecognisable. I may shoot him if he has got a gun. I expect he has, as he's too much of a coward to stand a thrashing . . . Of course I may get it in the neck first. You see I am quite cool. If that happens, oh, believe me, my own little darling . . . believe me it's for you. I swear to you I love you more than a man has loved a woman before . . . I thank [God] from the bottom of my heart for having sent me over in time to save you from this devil incarnate. Your honour is saved. Thank God, oh, thank God.

Goodbye, which means God be with you. I love you and shall go on loving you to eternity . . . I know I shall meet you in the next world if the worst happens, when you will come to me with open arms and those beautiful eyes shining, and say to me, Douggie – I forgive.

Yours for ever and ever, and oh so lovingly,

Your husband and very own

Douggie

Dorothy Taylor, before her marriage.

Lieutenant Malcolm had already provided himself with a horsewhip. And before going out, as his maid was to testify, he took his service revolver from the dressing-table drawer. It was still only eight in the morning when he reached a seedy boarding house in a street behind Paddington Station, a bare couple of miles in distance, but socially a whole world away.

He told the housemaid who opened the door that he was Inspector Quinn of Scotland Yard, and asked for the room of Anton Baumberg – or the Count de Borch, to use the alias by which every paper in the land was soon to know Mrs Malcolm's lover.

It was the worst room in the house, a top-floor back costing twelve shillings and sixpence a week, as Lieutenant Malcolm's defence counsel, Sir John Simon, said with some contempt.

The tenant in the next room, a female postal censor, described how she heard a violent quarrel and, a few minutes later, several shots. The *soi-disant* Count de Borch was dead.

Over the next few weeks, the court case at a packed Old Bailey that followed – one of the greatest human dramas ever staged, as the *Daily Sketch* described it – was to knock the war into second place on the front pages.

The three main protagonists – Lieutenant Malcolm, 'a man of antique honour', Dorothy Malcolm, 'a woman of great beauty' and Anton Baumberg, 'an adventurer of Russian-Polish (and

Jewish) extraction', were to become household names. Despite the tragedy, Douglas and Dorothy, my parents, remained married for the rest of their lives. I was born fifteen years later, their only child.

PART I

Dorothy Malcolm and Derek, 1933.

Dorothy Malcolm and Derek. Christening, 1932.

CHAPTER 1

ETON VS THE REST

Some people's secrets should never be told. The secret, though, that surrounded my parents' unhappy life together, and was suddenly divulged to me by accident, was so extraordinary that there seems no way of keeping it to myself now they are no longer alive. It has to be told, through the eyes of the only child who observed at first hand the wreckage it created of both their lives.

Like many personal tragedies, it carried with it considerable elements of farce, so that my parents sometimes became parodies of themselves and my own early life a kind of grim comedy too. Only when I finally solved the mystery was I able to understand that my own unhappiness was simply a reflection of theirs. They were two people who seemed to understand that their lives had been largely wasted, despite the considerable advantages of money and a position in society that should have allowed them more chances than most. They should never have been together in the first place but lacked the will to do something about it within a culture where divorce was still difficult and frowned upon.

7

They put me down for Eton before I was born. God knows what would have happened had I been a girl. It was really my mother's idea. My father preferred Uppingham, the public school to which he went, but acquiesced reluctantly, observing that if I was any good I could go into the Diplomatic Service and, if I wasn't, into the Cavalry 'where only the horses would notice'.

Eton in those post-war days meant a series of boarding schools, each a crammer for the next, starting in my case near the small country town of Burford in Oxfordshire at the tender age of four and ending at Summerfields on the outskirts of Oxford at the age of twelve. When I finally arrived at Eton, I felt rather as if I were going from one open prison to the next.

Summerfields was such a crammer for Eton that the midsummer sports day's tug-of-war contest was between those going to Eton and those unfortunate enough to be destined for lesser educational establishments. The Etonians invariably won, largely because there were so many more of them that even the masters recruited to help pull on the non-Etonian rope made no appreciable difference.

It was not a particularly happy progress for me at this virtually all-male, severely hierarchical educational establishment, which encouraged a kind of hardy Christianity and a pretty narrow, almost Victorian view of the correct behaviour in life. You were supposed at school to keep quiet, work hard and play harder. Individuality was frowned upon since it could lead to unorthodox thinking. Such places as Summerfields were not uncommon, catering for the upper middle classes, those with the money to aspire to them and the occasional foreign princeling. Money certainly let in the sons of some of the merely nouveau riche. But not too many. Most of us were from roughly the same background, though in my case the fact that my father had lost most of his money meant that I considered myself the slightly poor relation of my friends.

Added to that, I was small, asthmatic, timid at sports and academically without much confidence. It had taken me so long to learn to read that my father suggested I would be better off forgetting about books and learning to ride a horse, which I did with some relief.

Summer Fields, Near Oxford, School House.

It looked like the Cavalry for me, though when I finally learnt to read and write, I had taken it up with some enthusiasm. What I read wasn't much good – the top of the pile was probably C. S. Forester. But, in the absence of any guidance, I tried to improve myself and to stretch my imagination. Even so, it seemed unlikely to me, and highly unlikely to those who taught me Latin and Greek, that I would be much of a credit to a school which celebrated its distinguished old pupils as if they were at the right hand of God.

It wasn't the kind of early life in which my parents figured greatly, though they were always affectionate towards me and wrote to me regularly when I was away at school. They were simply not there for the greater part of the year, and when they were, it was clear that they didn't exactly relish the emotional work involved in succouring a child so late in life. My mother was over forty when she had me. My father was nearly fifty.

It was clear to me from a fairly early age, and certainly by the time I reached Summerfields, that the marriage had been irreparably damaged years before I was born. While it never looked like ending, it looked to me like, at best, an uneasy truce. At worst, it was out-and-out war. If I dreaded school, the holidays were not without their different traumas. Home was in one way a happy place since I was not being overseen by masters

10

who had a low opinion of me. But it was also unsettling. At the time, I had no idea why, except that my father seemed to prefer horses to humans, often saying he'd rather visit a vet when he was out of sorts than a doctor. My mother was the kind of person who loved the countryside provided you didn't open the windows of the car too often. They were entirely different people, constantly getting on each other's nerves but making an often abortive attempt to come together as parents. I couldn't imagine a time when it was otherwise.

All I remember about my first boarding school – what they used to call a kindergarten – was that I was almost always ill, and that it was run by two spinster sisters, the senior of whom once wrote to my parents, 'Derek is surprisingly well. He hasn't been sick for fully three weeks.' Generally it was asthma that laid me low, or coughs and colds, which developed into bronchitis.

The middle-aged and highly respectable sisters, who ran a kind of pre-school establishment for parents wanting to get rid of their offpring early so that they could pursue their lives in comparative peace, were kindly enough and anxious to show their young pupils the affection they craved. And the setting was fine, deep in the Cotswold countryside. But I wasn't very happy and can only remember the bad things about Cotter's Bow, such as being almost permanently weakly and being chased by an older boy with spiders, which induced a lifelong terror of them. The sight of a spider on the ceiling of my room was far worse than finding myself alone one day in a field with an enraged bull that caught me and threw me several feet into the air. Fortunately, the animal left me alone when I came down to earth, which my father said showed that I was too skinny to be eaten successfully.

He visited me occasionally, treated me with some kindness and usually took me out to tea in nearby Burford. My mother came down from London less often, though she smothered me with kisses when she did. But they seldom came together unless summoned by the doctor. They wrote postcards to me a lot, generally with just one sentence attached, like 'Isn't this a nice picture? Much love, Mummy' or 'Hope you are

Derek Malcolm,
aged 15 months
at Westgate-on-Sea.

keeping well. Love, Daddy'. I waited anxiously for the post every day.

There were other schools before Summerfields in Oxford but I can remember little about them, except that one of them was evacuated as a safety measure during the war from Bexhill-on-Sea on the Sussex coast to Bude in Cornwall many miles away, which meant that I hardly ever saw my parents in term time.

It was still wartime at Summerfields, and there was an air of desperate clinging on to former standards. The food in the big hall where the 120 or so boys ate was awful. I recall bread and dripping, very little butter or milk, owing to rationing, snoek steak (something like whale meat) in the absence of lamb or beef, watery cocoa in the evenings and vegetables invariably cooked out of all recognition. It was not the school's fault, though whoever did the cooking was hardly imaginative, even under the strained circumstances. Perhaps it was as well, as some nutritionists now say that the wartime diet left the young fitter than they are currently since it contained far less fat and chemicals. But it wasn't very nice to eat.

The masters were an odd assortment, made up of men who were either too old for the armed forces or not fit enough to be recruited. One or two of them we suspected to be German spies, perhaps because they had that shady look that betokens teaching as the last resort. Several of them had to be avoided as far as possible since they spent half their time tampering with the boys. We always tried to keep to windward of the elderly music teacher who, when the urge came upon him, took one or other of the younger of us on his lap, often in front of the whole class, put his hands in our trouser pockets and fiddled about with our genitals as we listened to the classical music he had selected on his gramophone. To this day, I can't hear Mendelssohn's *Fingal's Cave* without recalling the embarrassment of it all. But it was only embarrassment. I can't say we were either much shocked or traumatised. We giggled quietly to ourselves when it happened to someone other than ourselves.

We had to have cold baths every morning, winter and summer, since there were no showers at that time, and the music master, when conducting these daily rituals of torture, would stand with a switch in his hand and tap each of us on the bottom as we plunged in and out. It didn't give us as much pain as the cold water, but it clearly gave him some sort of pleasure. Ah, Mr Thompson, I remember you well!

There was one master, an excellent teacher and a kindly man, who never sent anyone to be beaten by the headmaster, but he was expelled, though we never knew to whom he did what. It was a very dark secret. He arrived back a year later, however, to receive an ovation from the entire school as he walked into the dinner hall. Which goes to prove that not all those who lusted after young boys were either very dangerous or even disliked for it. We knew what was likely to happen and became adept at avoiding too much proximity. We could not, though, avoid the headmaster, a clergyman who managed somehow to charm our parents but preserved a severe set face with the boys, as if he expected the worst and was usually right. In between giving us long and turgid sermons about sin in chapel, he used to enjoy beating bare-bottomed offenders either with a slipper or a cane. Or so it seemed to us. There was certainly a savage glint in his eyes as he did so, though he always professed deep regret at having to chastise us. He went at it with such a will that Matron often had to dab our rear ends with TCP.

Matron and her younger helper, and the maids who cleaned the school and laid out the meals, were the only females we ever saw. In general they seemed anxious not to get too fond of any of us in case the weaker, more homesick brethren got too fond of them. Nowadays, of course, the behaviour of some of the male members of staff would be the subject of both shock and concern. But at that time we took it all as just another of the more dangerous facets of boarding-school life. We never thought of complaining either to our parents or anyone else. In the former case, our parents might have taken us away and sent us somewhere even worse. In the latter, who was going to believe us if the culprits denied it?

15

If anything really untoward occurred, I never knew about it, and the prevailing atmosphere was strict and paternalistic. We were being taught securely middle-class standards and were expected to live up to them. Besides, many of us, in the general absence of girls, often had crushes on each other. Something sexual had to be expressed somehow.

The man we really feared, as it happened, was not a tamperer but, since he had been badly gassed in the First World War, had a temper that probably sprang from constant pain. He was a very tall, very skinny man of about sixty with a face that seemed like a skeleton with skin on it. He did not brook fools or idlers gladly. He was not impressed with my efforts at learning Ancient Greek, once scrawling three words across my annual report: 'Bloody idle swine.' This displeased my father greatly and he threatened to horsewhip him when he next caught sight of him. Fortunately, he never did. 'Poor little boy,' my mother said, 'But you really should try harder.'

Most of my reports were not as bad as that, but laid emphasis on my feeble efforts to be educated enough to pass into Eton and my hopelessness at sports, which might have helped my case in the absence of academic distinction. I was forced to be a hooker at rugby football, which meant being severely manhandled in the scrum by some of the most revolting thugs in the school. I was a goal-keeper at soccer, which was ludicrous since I was so small. On the cricket field I was the kind of team-mate who recoiled from taking catches because the ball was so hard. 'You're a funk, sir,' said one of the more sadistic masters every time I avoided the ball. Had he taught me how to catch it properly, I would soon have learnt that it didn't hurt so much.

We were constantly being told about the number of Victoria Crosses won by ex-Summerfieldians either in the First World War or the Second. We were even given a half-day off work to celebrate some award or other to a serving officer trained at Summerfields. To be a bloody idle swine was one thing, but to be labelled a coward was infinitely worse. I never quite got over it. My private prayers for rain on match days, answered quite frequently owing to the vagaries of the English summer, were a good deal more sincere than anything I managed when we prayed in unison in chapel. God, of course, was a major part of the syllabus at Summerfields and chapel was compulsory. If the Church of England was at that time considered to be the Conservative Party at prayer, there were a lot of young boys taught to grow up and equate the two, and to believe that life at school was a preparation for a life outside that wasn't fundamentally very different. The Bishop of Oxford paid us the occasional visit, and was received as if he were the Holy Ghost. The incense would swirl around the ugly Victorian-style chapel with its even uglier stained-glass windows until those with allergies started sneezing. All this religiosity led me towards an underclared agnosticism, balanced by the fear that the headmaster might be right and there was such a thing as hell. You had to hedge your bets, and when God delivered rain on sports days, I felt a vague hope that He existed.

Curiously, it wasn't Etonians versus the Rest that formed the pecking order among the boys. Instead, it was Cavaliers versus Roundheads. The names only indirectly referred to the supporters of King Charles and Oliver Cromwell. Roundheads were simply those who had been circumcised, and Cavaliers those who had not. I was a Roundhead but, with typical foolishness, attached myself to the Cavalier camp because I liked the thought of the attractive Charles rather than the warty Cromwell (a result probably of our conservatively inclined history lessons). I got the feeling that Cromwell would have called me an idle swine and a funk too. When I was found out, I was forcibly expelled from the Cavalier ranks. 'Once you're done, you're done,' said the leader of the Cavaliers. 'You can't stick your foreskin back on again even if you could find it.'

'How disgusting!' my mother said when she got wind of this. 'What will little boys think of next?' All my father would opine was, 'I told you not to have it done. It's unnecessary, and frightfully expensive as well.' Very painful too, I seem to remember. They took everything they could off or out in those days – foreskins, tonsils, appendices and in-growing toenails.

Knowing how many of the masters felt about the boys, it wasn't so surprising that we were wont to like each other almost as much as our teachers did. Not much was achieved sexually, but I do remember wondering whether I would ever begin to like those peculiar things called girls. One day, however, wandering in the woods near the school boundaries, I actually met one. She was standing by the fence that separated the bottom of her garden from the school playing fields. She was about my age and very pretty, and we just stared at each other for a bit without talking before she went back into the house and left me alone again. It became a regular meeting place for us – a kind of tryst of which it was clear that nothing would come. But we did get to talk, tentatively and with the attempt, on my part, to sound matter-of-fact. To my shame, I can't remember her name, but I think it was Rosemary. It was my first affair and we never touched each other. I dreamt of one day suddenly giving her a kiss, but I was too much of a funk for that. Thereafter, however, I determined I was not 'queer', even though it was not done to suggest that one didn't fancy the prettier younger boys.

Somehow or other I was eventually accepted for Eton, and left Summerfields, with its large playing fields on which I often used to wander alone, with some regret and even a few tears. It wasn't such an awful place once you understood how to negotiate it. Looking back, what it taught us was to keep quiet if you didn't agree with the philosophy it espoused, and that life afterwards should follow much the same pattern. Humour God and your country, and all would be well.

My mother was much relieved when I passed the Eton entrance exam. I was surprisingly good at Divinity, which had been shoved down my throat for so long. She had, I think, expected the worst. My father, mindful of the fees, would not have cared if I had gone elsewhere. He told me that it was cheaper to own and train a racehorse than to educate a boy at Eton. He stopped my piano lessons at Summerfields as an unnecessary extra – a fact I have deeply regretted for the rest of my life. 'That boy is very musical,' said Ellen Pollock, the actress friend of my mother, 'You must persuade his father to let him continue.' But my father was adamant. He couldn't afford it and that was that. No use at all, I suppose, in the Cavalry where he thought I would most probably end up.

I went to a house at Eton run by a veteran housemaster who didn't have much of a hold upon his hundred or so charges. He didn't seem to care much about what was going on as long as various sports trophies were won and the best brains got into university. But he soon retired and was succeeded by a younger man with a firmer grip on things. And the bullying, which was commonplace during my first year, was stopped.

As far as I was concerned it centred round one boy in particular who seemed to enjoy attempting to crush the personalities of those younger boys with whom he deigned to associate. He wasn't a senior but a junior just in advance of our new lot, and he was clearly a sadist of some sort, since his favourite trick was to mix up cold cream with his own excrement and then make the new boys eat it. But I refused and employed the only means of defence I knew, which was to mock him behind his back. Once people started to laugh at him, he ceased the worst of his activities, and kept well away from me, the begetter of the jokes. The last time I heard of him he was a successful solicitor in Sussex, proving to me that the bad prosper and the good often don't. I even wrote a piece about him many years later in the *Guardian*. When the editor read it, he told me he hoped I hadn't given him his real name. Actually, I had, and apparently he had read it, with considerable mortification. Revenge seemed very sweet at the time.

The advantage of Eton over most other public schools in those days was the fact that even the newest new boy had a room of his own with a desk, a bed and a couple of chairs. You got a better room the longer you stayed. You were assigned a fagmaster and were thus his fag – an unfortunate term perhaps, but a way of getting to know one of the older boys who would expect you to make his bed, keep his room tidy, light his coal fire in the

21

winter and run errands for him. Certain senior boys were allowed an additional favour. They could open the door of their room and shout 'Boy!' as loud and as long as they could make the word sound. Whereupon the junior boys would have to come running. The last of them was sent on the errand, perhaps to another house, which wasn't as easy as it may sound. If you failed, you could be reported to the Library, which was composed of the top few boys in the house and was a room lined with books and papers, and dotted with wicker chairs. I was wont, through sheer lack of speed, to be last in the queue when 'Boy!' was called and thus had a good many messages to deliver. This was difficult, because I could not for some time work out which house was where. They were always identified merely by the initials of the housemaster on the folded note you had to deliver. 'Take this to Cunningham Major at CJR's,' the senior boy would say and woe betide you if you couldn't find it or him. Fagging, however, was not too much of a pain when you got to know the rules, especially when your fagmaster was a kindly sort. Most of mine were. And luckily none of them had designs on me sexually. Illicit activity between an older and a younger boy was not entirely unknown and, though frowned upon, was not thought the most deadly of sins. During my time at Eton a prominent member of Pop, the select society who had risen above the rest of us and were allowed to wear flowered waist-coats and call for fags wherever they liked, was found, presumably in flagrante, with one of the maids in his house. Although it was his last term, and he was due to go to Cambridge, he was instantly stripped of his Pop outfit and expelled from the school. Had he been found with one of the younger boys, we all felt, he would merely have been reprimanded. But then, as a member of our Library once said to me, 'Little boys for fun, women for serious business.'

Derek Malcolm in
Eton 'Bum-freezer'.

I remember keeping a calendar pinned up on the inside of the desk in my room on which I ringed the days during which I committed the dastardly act of masturbation. It was a generally futive attempt to ration myself and I have to confess there were some days when a double ring was indicated. However, I was sometimes successful and occasionally a whole week went by without a ring round any of the seven days. Generally, though, I considered two rings good, three fair and five awful. But I was exceedingly proud when the time came for me to be confirmed. There were no rings at all the whole week before the confirmation, and none for two whole weeks afterwards. Alas, on the third week I rose again, and the rings appeared with monotonous regularity. I cannot now imagine why I felt that I had to abstain during this period but momentarily felt very pleased with myself.

It was sometimes difficult since I suspected that my friends were probably having more sexual fun than me, particularly a stout boy called Barford and a very pretty boy called Judd who was desired by almost everybody. Somehow or other Barford, a real lech, had made friends with Judd and used to visit him in the room directly above mine. What they did together I have no real idea, but one summer's night when the windows were open I heard the words, repeated again and again: 'Oh, Judd! Oh, Barford! Oh, Judd! Oh, Barford!'. It was the most erotic moment of my life thus far.

Fortunately, however, I never got hold of Judd myself. Instead, I rather fancied the maid on our landing who occasionally used to invite me into her room for tea. Nothing happened except in my imagination.

Being small and weedy, I remained a little boy for a long time. You had to wear what were known as bum-freezers, a short coat and a larger, stiff collar until you were the height required to be allowed soft collars and tailcoats (which made you look more like a waiter than Little Lord Fauntleroy). This was a grave handicap, since I was regarded as a Lower Boy longer than most and was assailed by those who fancied me for longer than was usual. As at Summerfields, nothing much happened. I did, though, have a fagmaster who tried to get into my room one night but withdrew quickly when I objected. He probably thought I was thirteen, not fifteen. When I finally got into my tails and threw my bum-freezers away, I was mightily pleased.

My career at Eton, however, was not much of an improvement on Summerfields. Writing to my father in August 1946, my housemaster said,

> Dear Malcolm,
> I am afraid you will not think much of Derek's reports. . . . he seems to have given way to a weakness of will and lack of determination to succeed. His masters like him well, but his childishness exasperated Mr

Hedley particularly. I really do think it is time he began to grow up. He is too nice to get into any serious trouble but he has little sense of responsibility or personal dignity. Anything that could be done to let him on his own – a long journey, all worked out by himself, for instance – would, I am sure, give him some of the poise which, perhaps owing to his small stature, he so sadly lacks. It is no fault of his that he is not likely to be distinguished at Eton, but among a lot of energetic and enthusiastic boys, he might come to be regarded as something of a loafer. I must repeat, there is no vice in him; but that is very negative praise.

 With all good wishes,
  James Parr

Parr was a big, fleshy man of around forty, with a permanently red face, either caused by drink or blood pressure but probably both. He wasn't at all a bad man but his summing up of my character, which I claimed to my parents was totally wrong, remained under my skin for a long time. No real good at class work, certainly no good at team sports, was an unfortunate tag to live with at school. But I did have some minor triumphs. My school friends thought me amusing, especially mimicking either the housemaster or the other boys. I did an excellent

Churchill, for instance, and a very passable King George and Princess Margaret, though I couldn't fart 'God Save the King' as well as one of my friends. People came into my room for a good laugh. And eventually I made myself into a passable tennis, squash and fives player, taking the greatest delight in beating Mr Parr in a game of squash. 'Derek', he wrote to my father, 'has surprised me by becoming a very decent squash and tennis player. I am pleased for him, since his lack of distinction in almost every other way must have disappointed you as much as it has myself.'

The omens were not promising for Oxford, where my mother was determined I should go, and Parr duly wrote to my parents, 'Derek is very unlikely to benefit much from university, even if he were lucky enough to get in, which I'm afraid I doubt. Might I suggest the Army, or possibly farming? Neither of these might prove too difficult for him.'

His wife, a small, very ladylike and attractive woman, who looked as though she'd been smothered regularly by her large husband, disagreed with the general tone of his remarks. 'There's something about your boy,' she said to my parents once when they visited. 'He's got a definite personality and talent. But for the life of me, I'm not sure what it is. I had him to dinner with some other adult guests the other week, and I found they were all listening to him intently. He has a gift with words, and a rather lovely voice. Maybe he is a late developer and it will all come out eventually.'

The only person who did detect some talent in me was another housemaster who taught me English, cast me in plays he produced (generally in one of the female parts with a wig) and amazed my own housemaster by saying I might one day become a writer. He was clearly a homosexual and I suspect was rather fond of me, but he was always discreet. The first time he gave me full marks for an essay was, however, rather shaming. I had copied it straight from the work of Jerome K. Jerome, the author of *Three Men in a Boat*. On top of the first page, he wrote, '10 out of 10. If original, most original.'

He cast me as Vera Claythorne in Agatha Christie's *Ten Little Niggers* – the title had not been changed to *And Then There Were None* by then. The big moment came when the hero of the piece had to embrace me in the final scene. The wig slipped off as he kissed me. There was a howl of joy from the audience of boys and masters that I will remember all my life. But the master who had encouraged me so much sent me a note the next day: 'Sorry about the accident. But you were very good indeed. As good, in fact, as anyone else and possibly better.'

It was he, and he alone, who gave me some confidence, although the way I had managed to deal with the sadistic budding solicitor earned some credit among my contemporaries. I added to my score by being birched by the Lower Master – a feat I achieved for persistently talking in chapel and, in particular, completing the prayer 'Matthew, Mark, Luke and John guard the bed that I lie on. There are two angels at its head . . .' with the words, 'There's one of them I'd like IN bed.'

The birching ceremony was designed to terrify more than to injure, though invariably blood was drawn. The offender was summoned to a building in the main quad and waited shakily outside until a stentorian voice shouted 'Enter!'. He was then told to kneel down on an ancient wooden block, beside which two college servants were standing. Once on the block, the servants took down his trousers and pants, and the Lower Master stepped forward with the birch. The servants held the boy down between the arms. The Lower Master was a nice old man, as it happens, who clearly did not relish this part of his duties. Observing my smallness and fright, he proceeded to give me six strokes which could hardly have been much softer. I was then told to get up, go back to class and stop talking in chapel. 'What if God heard you?' said the Lower Master in a tone of kindly regret as I hauled up my trousers.

Derek Malcolm,
finally in tails, at
Eton on the
Fourth of June.

Not many received this treatment even in my day, and when I got back to the classroom there was a buzz of excitement. My fellows thought I might be unable to sit down. But I did and later showed them the blood on my pants. It was the first and only time I seemed like a hero at Eton. Later, my mother rang up and asked to speak to me on the phone, rather ruining it all by exclaiming, 'Oh, what a naughty boy! Is diddums all right, then?' That is not what you want to hear at the age of fourteen, and I hastily explained that the blood was still flowing.

Much worse than the birching, however, was the terror of being summoned to the Library. There a group of the five or six senior boys in the house were allowed to loiter and keep discipline by beatings, if necessary. This was done at night after we had all gone to our rooms – there were no dormitories at Eton, the one advantage, I thought, of being there. You would hear one of the seniors marching along the corridor, hoping he wouldn't stop at your door and knock. If he did, you opened it to hear, 'Come down to the Library and wait outside.' You would then wait outside the Library until summoned again. When you entered, the head boy was standing there, cane in hand. The rest were seated in chairs around the room, pretending to be reading the papers (they were not allowed by house rules to look). 'Malcolm,' the head boy would then say, 'your fagmaster has informed me that you failed to light his fire by 4 p.m. – not once but twice. Have you anything to say?'

'No sir.'

'Very well, you will be beaten. Bend down.' He was not allowed to take your trousers off and it was thus the practice to stuff them with either newspaper or cardboard in order to take the worst sting off the punishment. I favoured the *Racing Calendar* myself. But often the head boy twigged after the first stroke that something was protecting the offender and laid in harder and more often in consequence. After which he said, 'You may go,' and you returned, often tearfully, to your room.

Beating by cane hurt far more than the birch, but the worst thing of all was waiting for the footsteps outside your door before the torture began.

It was supposed to be carefully regulated by your housemaster, from whom the head boy had to get permission. I've no doubt it was in most houses, but not in mine. The nature of the beating was determined by the predilections of the head boy – one of whom took a great dislike of a friend of mine called Wheeler, whose obstinate refusal to be cowed led to a great many harder and harder beatings. I imagine the process must have affected him for the rest of his life.

Parents were invariably told of the disgrace of birchings but not of house beatings, except in the case of persistent offenders in the end-of-term report. Mine seldom visited except on the Fourth of June, Eton's great day in the summer term, when my father would arrive with my mother in a grubby old Ford Popular to watch the cricket. He would drive it into the car park among the newly polished, frequently chauffeur-driven Bentleys, complaining bitterly about how much space they took up. He always wore his grey suit, pulled out of a cupboard unironed and not quite clean. My mother made her entrance in her very considerable Harrods best, aghast at appearing like poor relations down for the day. Though approaching sixty, she was still a beautiful and elegant woman. My father had a certain something about him, but it was not evident in the cut of his clothes. I was usually worried that they would either quarrel or make fools of themselves. Others no doubt felt the same way about their parents. Few are ever proud of them. But I had more reason than most to agonise.

One year, it started to rain and my father pulled out of the car a multicoloured umbrella which, when unfurled, read 'Prince Monolulu for the Best Tips.' I nearly died of shame, though now I admire his cussedness. He had been given the umbrella by the famous black tipster at Goodwood, apparently after the Prince had lost his betting slip. A long time later, at Ascot, I actually met Prince Monolulu, who claimed to be descended from a princely family in Nigeria. He remembered my father and immediately asked whether he'd still got his umbrella. There was a pub named after the Prince at the top of Charlotte Street in London, an honour he deserved for enlivening so many meetings with his plumed and caparisoned presence.

There was another tipster my father and I knew, who went under the name of Gully Gully. Gully Gully wore a brown suit, a pork pie hat and an Old Etonian tie. He had a very red face like my housemaster. If you exhibited the tie too, which I occasionally did, he would rush up to you and say, 'And which house were you at, sir?' Whatever you replied, he'd exclaim, 'Good lord, so was I! Now have I gotta horse for you!' He would charge £1 and slip you the horse's name on a piece of paper. Of course, he never went to Eton, but his cheek was catching and, what's more, his tips often won. 'Told you so!' he'd shout if he saw you after the race. 'There's nothing like doing a favour for an old school friend . . .'

CHAPTER 2

MANNERS MAKETH MANNERS

My parents were no longer rich but nothing like as poor as my father pretended. There was still enough capital to produce a reasonable income. My father ascribed his financial fate to my mother's extravagance. My mother reckoned his own unwise investments were the cause: 'Douglas was never any good with money.' The truth lay somewhere between the two. My mother ran up bills at Harrods which were indeed unwise, and my father's capacity to make £100 into £10 on the Stock Exchange within the shortest possible time was legendary. He laid claim to be the most unfortunate gambler in the world, prone to pitch in regardless once he was given a tip, generally from someone no one else would consider reliable. He had let slip most of a large fortune in this way by the time I was born, not helped by the Depression years. And, though well-lined enough never to have to take a job in his life, he refused to believe he was not a pauper, fighting off imminent bankruptcy. I was taught from an early age that to spend money was a foolish activity. 'Money saved

34

is money gained,' was his watchword. To leave the boiler on when you didn't need a bath was a cardinal sin and electric or gas fires and lights were there to be turned off rather than on.

I can't say I knew him very well during the first years of my life, which were spent either at school or in a flat at Ashley Court, over-looking Westminster Cathedral. There I lived with my mother but not with my father, who merely visited from time to time. I had no idea where he lived, but it was somewhere he could hunt three times a week. He treated me with the kind of rough affection he would show to one of his favourite horses. In contrast to my mother, he was unable to show much real emotion. But, however awkwardly expressed, his affection was constant.

My mother's was fulsome but apt to be inconsistent. She had many friends. A lot of them were men. I had nannies to look after me when I wasn't at school and was hustled away as soon as company arrived. If I was allowed to stay in the room, they all spoke in cracked French if anything indelicate was being discussed, which it often was. The reason I did passably well in French lessons was simply to be able to find out what my mother and her friends were talking about. It was almost always sex. Other people's affairs.

I was seven when war broke out, and used to look out of my bedroom window terrified that a bomb would hit the cathedral and that the brick spire would fall on the flat. When the Blitz began in earnest, I was taken down to the shelter by my mother who by this time had volunteered as an Air Raid Warden, summoning one and all to keep their curtains closed and lights off during raids.

The one thing I remember about those times was a tough-looking, middle-aged American called Victor sitting on the side of my bed and telling me stories to get me to sleep. Afterwards, I discovered it was Victor McLaglan, the Hollywood actor who was a regular in John Ford's Westerns, generally as the tough, loyal and no-nonsense soldier under the command of John Wayne. He seemed very fond of my mother. But so were a lot of men. She was still very handsome in middle age, despite frequently saying that suckling me had been the ruination of her breasts. But she could charm most men out of their skin and, for all I knew, out of their trousers.

She didn't seem to me, however, to be a particularly sexual person. More like someone in desperate need of constant admiration and possibly unconditional love. Whether she could return such love, for all her considerable charm and personal warmth, was more doubtful. In my case she tried, when she could remember. I was never quite certain whether I would be cuddled half to death or ignored.

She seemed always to be short of money but had a cleaner called Mrs Perkins who came to Ashley Court regularly and eventually got herself pregnant. To my mother's initial horror, she called the baby Adolf 'because he was born in the Blitz'. We laughed about this a lot and it was laughter which bound me to my mother more than anything. She was an excellent mimic and did Mrs Perkins, telling us about little Adolf, extremely well. None of her 'servants' escaped this process but, though it would be thought highly incorrect today, one never felt there was much of a sneer in her comic imitations.

My parents started to live together again when it was decided to leave London for Bexhill-on-Sea. They found a small, balconied house right on the seafront with a flat roof upon which a bomb landed, fortunately without exploding, almost as soon as we moved in. The result was startling since my father had only just got out of the bed a moment before the ceiling collapsed on it.

His war effort was confined, after he returned from France via Dunkirk with several bottles of French brandy, to the Home Guard. 'I hope they frighten Hitler,' he observed, 'because they certainly frighten me.' My mother volunteered once again, this time for the St John Ambulance Brigade, though objecting strenuously to 'this dreadful uniform we have to put on'. I don't think she was very good at first aid but fairly proficient at being the grand lady pretending to command the Bexhill branch of the Brigade.

At this time we had three servants, though there was hardly room for six people in the house, plus my mother's greyhound called Seppi, apparently the offspring of the greyhound Derby winner, Mick The Miller. During the school holidays I was relegated to a made-up bed on the sitting-room sofa because of the crush. At one point we had a butler-cum-general factotum called Manners. Mrs Manners was cook-housekeeper and Rita, their nubile daughter, was the maid. They ruled the roost in an offhandedly respectful kind of way.

Manners would wait at table with a somewhat grudging demeanour. He called me Master Derek and seldom spoke directly to me. 'And would Master Derek like some more porridge?' he would say to my mother as if I weren't there. She would then ask me, I would reply and she would repeat what I had said to Manners. He called her 'Madam' and my father 'Captain' – the rank he had achieved by the end of the First World War. Manners was inclined to be irascible, judging by the rows he had with Mrs Manners, which I sometimes overhead. And he considered cleaning my father's hunting boots beyond the call of duty. Matters came to a head early one morning over this part of his duties when my father called out from just outside his bedroom door, 'Manners, where are my boots?' Whereupon Manners marched upstairs, threw them at the door and shouted, 'Clean your own bloody boots!' When told of this recalcitrance, my mother laughed heartily but admonished Manners in as serious a tone as she could muster, 'Manners maketh Manners, Manners.' 'Sorry, madam,' he replied,

38

'but my patience was temporarily exhausted. Had the Captain asked me to polish his boots the night before, I would have gladly done so as usual. Unfortunately he did not. If he fails to tell me, I'm afraid I cannot guess when he is off hunting.'

Mrs Manners, a fat lady whose struggle to get up the stairs was always accompanied by heavy sighs, would knock on my mother's bedroom door shortly after breakfast to discuss the day's menus with her – not usually a very long discussion during the war, since there wasn't much to be had and someone had invariably lost their ration book.

Rita busied herself with the housework, keeping a wary eye on me, who tended to keep an eye on her for reasons she rightly felt might be a little suspect. She was the kind of buxom girl I could never get hold of at Bexhill-on-Sea. It appeared to me, probably wrongly, that the higher up the social pecking order the girls I was allowed to associate with, the less prominent were their breasts. And those with double-barrelled names, quite common in those days, often had none to speak of. Single-barrelled chests, in fact.

We had a small garden right on the seafront bordering the Bexhill Promenade, which was wired up owing to the threat of imminent invasion. Having left London because of the Blitz, it seemed peculiar to land up in place that could have been infinitely more dangerous. It was rather like my father backing the wrong horses at the races or the wrong shares on the Stock Exchange, even if it was generally thought likely that nearby Pevensey Bay might be the actual site of any German landing. This was where my father kept his last horse, a skinny and bad-tempered animal one did not feel would be able to delay the enemy for long.

The nearest we came to real danger was when German bombers, having roared over the area on their way to London, would jettison their spare bombs on the way back. 'Don't go out on the balcony, dear,' my mother would say. 'You never know what may fall on your head.' None of this deflected my father from his regime of keeping fit by bathing in the sea. As he said, 'Bugger the war.' He managed to cut his way through the wire and plunge into the water in winter as well as summer, regardless of the weather, which could be bitter, with winds that cut through you like a knife. I used to watch the intrepid walkers, once the war was over, struggling along the Promenade, bent forward as they battled one way and backwards as they were blown the other. During the war, however, there was no one at all to be seen from our balcony.

There was, though, one uninvited guest. While we were having breakfast one morning, Manners walked in with the fish kedgeree and calmly announced, 'Captain, a German airman has just parachuted into the garden. He seems to have hurt himself so he won't move far. May I have your instructions?'

'Bloody nuisance,' my father replied, peering outside. 'I suppose we'd better send for the police.'

'Take the poor man a cup of tea,' my mother said. Both of them went straight back to the dining table, nor did the incident interrupt their breakfast for more than a minute or so, even though the stricken enemy lay sprawled on the daffodils scarcely ten yards away from the french windows. It was a bit like the scene in *Carry On Up the Khyber* when the Brits calmly eat dinner as the natives get increasingly restless outside the compound and their shelling plays havoc with the dining-room ceiling and chandeliers.

The police arrived with an ambulance and carted the poor man away, without either my Home Guard father or my St John Ambulance Brigade mother so much as leaving the room – a dereliction of duty I found amazing at the time but thought afterwards was a rather fine piece of sang-froid. Manners dealt with it all. 'I think he'll be all right, Captain,' he said. 'His parachute saved him, you understand. But I can't say the same, I'm afraid, for the daffodils.'

My mother was content to observe, 'One really doesn't know what will happen next these days.'

Nor did I. But I wasn't much frightened by the thought of an invasion since my father constantly remarked that 'Hitler wouldn't dare.' Besides, he added, the Führer rather liked the English and admired their phlegm. 'He's Austrian, you know, not German,' he used to add, as if that made some difference.

It was not, however, an easy household in which to grow up. Now they were living together, it was patently obvious that my father and mother were partners forged in purgatory if not in hell. All I wished, when they were at their worst, was that they would part company, for my sake as well as their own. Until they grew too old to care, which eventually did happen, there was always the prospect of a sudden eruption of temper in between pregnant silences. Though each tried sporadically to gain my support, they revealed nothing much of themselves. At that time I had no idea what had brought them together in the first place, or what kept them together for so long in the second.

There is a single tower, like the castle in a chess set, carved on the backs of the old ivory brushes my father used to have on his dressing table, and I still have on mine. The motto underneath the towers is 'In Ardua Tendit', of which a free translation might be 'What I have I hold'. That hardly applied to my branch of the Malcolm clan, which seemed to be able to hold practically nothing they owned for very long. They went from poor to rich to poor again for some 250 years. By the time my father died, he had managed to convert some £450,000 in 1932 to £35,000 in the early nineteen seventies.

The Malcolms of Poltalloch were able to rejoice

in the motto as Scottish landed gentry since the middle of the sixteenth century when, in 1562, Donald McGillespie mac O'Challum was granted the property of Poltalloch on the western shore of Argyll, facing the beautiful windswept islands of Jura and Mull across the water. The family gravestones in the church at Kilmartin go back even earlier. But by the middle of the eighteenth century the clan had fallen on hard times within a generally impoverished land, and it was only a chance inheritance of estates in Jamaica that set Dugald Malcolm on the path that restored the family fortunes through slaves and rum. From then onwards the family's time was largely spent south, in London or abroad, purchasing land in Australia and Canada as well as in Kent.

Even so their emotional links to Scotland seldom faltered. 'Malcolm of Poltalloch, the Croesus of Argyll,' wrote Lord Cockburn in 1841, and he noted that the house of Poltalloch itself was the visiting place of as many distinguished people as any in Edinburgh. It was Neill Malcolm who built it as 'an enormous private palace', designed in Jacobean style by William Burn with garden house and servants' library set in an estate that ran to some 85,000 acres for some 40 miles along the coast.

The family were still well-lined enough by the turn of the twentieth century to sell sixteen Leonardos, twenty-seven Raphaels and thirty Michelangelos in the drawing collection to the

British Museum for a purely nominal sum. The Sforza Book of Hours was donated as a gift. Mary Malcolm, the television personality, wrote in the late fifties of pre-Second World War childhood holidays in 'this private hotel' which, from early August to the end of September, had each of its twenty-five bedrooms full. A piper was accustomed to walk the passages to awaken guests to yet another long day of sport, and King Feisal of Iraq, planning to stay there after the state visit of 1933, told friends that he was 'going north to visit the tribes'.

But the sale of land, denoting yet another period of decline, had begun even as life at the house reached its pitch of prosperity. There were twenty-one women working inside the house at the turn of the century and forty-five estate tradesmen. By the outbreak of the First World War the numbers had dwindled considerably. After peace was declared the end, as for so many grand houses, came quickly. Properties in Jamaica and elsewhere were sold off in the forties and fifties, the family withdrew to smaller houses in the same neighbourhood and a buyer was sought for Poltalloch itself. When none was found, the roof was taken off in 1957 to avoid rates. The house became a ruin, with ferns growing in the fireplaces. 'Gutted, creeper-hung, enormous in scale . . . the image of noble decay could not have been more grand, sad or impressive than this noble pile,' wrote a local historian.

The Poltalloch fortune dwindled at roughly the same time as did those of my father's branch of the family. The traceable history of my father's family goes back to the second half of the last century when his grandfather and great-uncle went to London to make their fortune. They did so rapidly.

Poltalloch House.

James Robert Malcolm, my grandfather, was born in 1839, the son of a Dundee solicitor who died early, leaving his widow and five children in straitened circumstances. James, however, was able to finish his education in France and Germany before finding employment in Robinson, Fleming and Co., in which his brother William was a junior partner. They left together to found a jute business with offices in London and Dundee. By the end of the century they had opened branches in St Petersburg and Ostrov, Hamburg and Riga. But within a few years the successful operation was hit by the Russian Revolution. According to the firm's history, 'The upcountry native personnel disappeared like chaff in the wind.' The First World War, however, with its seemingly insatiable demand for jute sandbags, compensated considerably. Sisal from the Bahamas, and flax from East Africa and India led to the creation of more branches of the Malcolm firm in Bologna, New York and Madras.

Poltalloch House, entrance hall.

From the time my father was born in London in 1883, through his education at Uppingham, he had little choice but to join his father and elder brothers in the family firm. But he was clearly never suited to the life. He was a handsome, rugby-playing, military-orientated hunting man who had been given a considerable sum of money on his twenty-first birthday by his father and who cared very little for business in general or the jute trade in particular. He would have preferred a life of moneyed leisure with the study of butterflies and stamps as hobbies. He was, however, bound to the firm his generous father had expected him to join and honourably waited to resign until the old man died. The firm's historian claimed my father left 'following a disagreement with the other partners', but it looks as if the firm was as glad to be rid of him as he was to be shot of them. Before he resigned, a letter home from Calcutta, where he had been posted for a spell, summed up his attitude to the work and his unfamiliar surroundings: 'Slight attack of fever . . . pretty miserable lying in bed with a lot of barefoot niggers around you . . .'

He met my mother in London shortly after his return. The Douglas Malcolm of those days was, according to the photographs of the time, a handsome man with a slightly military demeanour who clearly knew his place in society and was determined to keep it. By the time we came to Bexhill he was almost sixty, smoked a pipe ceaselessly and dressed in clothes, sometimes including plus-fours or jodhpurs, that had clearly been bought expensively but which by now had seen better days. They almost always needed cleaning, and seldom got it. As soon as the war was over, he spent his days either hunting, playing golf or at bridge. He read a lot, too, in his favourite armchair, mostly the memoirs of generals and the like. He despised novels, though he did not disapprove of my initial passion for the historical fictions of G. A. Henty.

There was not much conversation to be had with him, though he tried as hard as he was able both to amuse or engage me on occasion. It was as though he were totally immersed in a world of his own, rising from it either to bicker with my mother or make awkward attempts to talk to me. It was rarely a success and we would relapse into silence fairly quickly. I don't think I behaved very well with him, since he considered Churchill virtually a God, the Duke of Edinburgh enormously intelligent and didn't like either Jews or those who voted for 'that ghastly little man Attlee'. This did not endear him to me, who cheered the post-war Labour victory, thought the Duke rather like the master at school who had called me a bloody idle swine and believed Attlee the sort of politician who brilliantly belied his mouselike looks. As for Jews, I was inclined to envy them as cleverer than myself and certainly more able to deal with life in general.

My father, though, was neither a high Tory nor a racist at heart, even if he seemed like one to me at the time. Years later, I insisted on taking him to a meet in my first car with a Labour sticker blazoned across the back window. 'Do take it off,' he said. 'It's most embarrassing for me.'

'Why should I?' I complained. 'It's my car.'

He seemed to realise I was more like my mother than him, though she too would never have voted Labour. I looked very like her physically, and people used sometimes to laugh at the resemblance when we were out walking together. I rather admired the stoic grace with which he took the fact that I wasn't 'his sort' at all. We were fond of each other, though to say so was more than either of us would have dared. When he kissed me on seeing me home again for the holidays from boarding school, it was as if he were gingerly nuzzling a horse.

I remember once journeying with him to Hampshire by train to visit some relatives. We started off alone in the carriage and remained so the whole way. This was because he would lean out of the window at every station and make peculiar faces at people waiting on the platform. They clearly thought it inadvisable, and possibly dangerous, to join us. He did this to stop people entering our carriage but also to keep me amused. He would frequently go out shopping with his flies undone – a fact no one dared to point out except the local fishmonger who would say, 'There's a slight gap in your trousers again this morning, Captain. Was it cod or kippers today?' He would take his daily dip in the sea, not in swimming trunks but in his frequently ragged underwear.

Those passing by looked diplomatically away. He seemed either to ignore the world or in some way to object to it. Once, dragged by my mother to a piano recital in London by the great Alfred Cortot, he shouted at the pianist during the usual pause between the movements of a sonata, 'Oh, get on with it, man!' Generally, however, he wasn't the slightest bit interested in the arts and seemed to despise all painters unless their subjects were horses or hounds.

But those who got to know him seemed prepared to forgive him almost anything. 'It's only the Captain,' was a phrase I heard more than once at Bexhill. I often wondered how I could be in his company without anyone realising he was my father. Now, of course, I wish I had been with him more. He was invariably true to himself, which is more than can be said for most people.

My mother was younger, but since she had given birth to me at the age of forty-two, not all that much. She kept her age a state secret. All I knew about her, as a child, was that she came from a family who lived in Muswell Hill in London, had a brother who died in the First World War and two sisters who had neither her beauty nor talent. It was only many years later that I began to fill in the blanks.

She was born Dorothy Vera Taylor in Gunnersbury, the daughter of Frederick Taylor, a solicitor with unfulfilled ambitions to become the Conservative candidate for either this con- stituency or Muswell Hill where they moved. She was one of four children – a boy and three girls – and by some way the best endowed for success in life. Not only was she beautiful but she had a fine if largely untrained contralto voice. She care- fully preserved into old age a letter from a tutor at the Royal College of Music testifying that 'Miss Dorothy Taylor's contribution to the world of music could be extraordinary'. Toscanini was said to have heard her sing and offered to take her off to Rome and train her for free. Without question, her beauty and her voice could have made her a star, at least of operetta, but her physical attrac- tions might possibly have had something to do with her tutor's enthusiasm and Toscanini's compliments, since a whole succession of men professed to adore her. As Sonia Seton, the name she adopted for her stage work, she appeared both as an actress and a singer in London and else- where, once playing the title role in Webster's *The Duchess of Malfi* for the famous producer Nigel Playfair in Oxford. She also appeared on the radio for the BBC.

Whether the development of her undoubted talents was stunted by her romance with and even- tual marriage to my father is a moot point. More likely, even before she knew him, she came to move in social circles way beyond the aspirations of anyone else in her family, and avoided the hard work a musical or stage career would entail. To be thought 'artistic' was considered decent enough for an upper-middle-class woman. To be some sort of entertainer was not. Or so she may have thought. She was also lazy, preferring the admiration of society and an easier life. 'Dorothy', observed an acquaintance before she met my father, 'prefers to luxuriate in compliments than to better herself intellectually, or even to make the most of her talents. She's a beautiful gadfly, pursued mostly by other gadflies, going who knows where.'

Both her sisters, Ida and Phyllis, were fond of her but furiously jealous too. The family realised that she could advance further than they could in the society of the day and let her have her head as the eldest child. She moved in ever grander circles as a London beauty of the day, concentrating, because of her singing ability, on those who were a good deal less hidebound by a Scottish clan's traditions than the James Douglas Malcolm who was to be her husband.

My father treated the Bohemian set with suspicion. He was largely uncultured, though by no means lacking in sensitivity behind that mask of vaguely aristocratic respectability which was the mark of the upper-middle-class Scots at the time. He fell instantly for Dorothy the moment he saw her at a Claridge's reception, pushed his way past several other admirers, invited her out to dinner and proceeded, according to my mother, to play footsie with her under the table. It wasn't long before he proposed, saying he had never met a woman so beautiful and 'so pure'. She thought about it for a bit and then accepted. After all, he was rich, handsome, well-connected and clearly adored her. She would never have to work but she could continue singing and acting at her leisure. She was probably not actually in love with my father, but certainly grew fond both of him and what he represented. It seemed like a fair match and the families were delighted. Only one friend sent her a letter advising against tying the knot. Still, perhaps my father could be trained or, if not, would allow her to go her own way. He would probably prefer a country life while she was in town . . .

Dorothy Malcolm(on balcony) as the Duchess in *The Duchess of Malfi* at Oxford.

The wedding took place at St Peter's, Eaton Square, on 23 June, 1914, with the bridegroom's clergyman brother-in-law performing the ceremony. A few weeks later, Douglas Malcolm volunteered for the war.

The marriage of Dorothy Taylor to Douglas Malcolm, 23 June, 1914.

Thirty years later I realised just how talented my mother was. Visiting me at school and attending the obligatory chapel service, she would cause half the congregation to turn round to see who was singing. She had a voice like an angel and could clearly have forged herself a considerable career. If, however, my father chose the wrong shares, she chose the wrong men, including him.

She used to take me up to London sometimes to do some shopping at stores like Harrods, which still allowed her an account, and to see a show, in particular the musicals of Ivor Novello, which she booked partly to enjoy them but partly also to indulge in the fantasy that, if she sat in the front row, the handsome matinée idol would notice her. Since he was clearly gay, I felt this a useless occupation but said nothing until, after one of his shows, she whispered to me, 'Did you see him staring at me during the second act?'

'Actually, mummy,' I said, with all the experience of private school behind me, 'he was probably looking at me.'

On another occasion, we went to the London Coliseum to see my particular favourites – Stan Laurel and Oliver Hardy. It was a mouthwatering variety bill, which also included Elsie and Doris Waters, two endearing comediennes in wartime headbuns whose act consisted of rambling conversations about all and sundry, almost always over a soothing cup of tea. There was also Rawicz and Landauer, a piano duo who played the classical standards side by side with the most popular light music of the day. But it was Laurel and Hardy I really wanted to see, veterans now and past their heyday, who were on a stage tour of England at the time. Returning from school at Victoria Station, I would often take time to go to the newsreel cinema there where, more often than not, a Laurel and Hardy short would be on the programme. I adored them and was upset to see a scattered, half-full house for the matinée. They were not totally comfortable doing their act on stage. It was as if they needed a camera to flourish properly. Even so, Olly's double takes were as magnificent as ever and Stan cried with complete conviction when he considered Olly had slighted him. When they hit each other with their hats, it was as brilliantly timed as always. I was spellbound.

At the interval I asked my mother if I could meet them, not very hopeful of any favourable result. But she upped from her seat and requested to see the manager. To my surprise and joy, at the end of the show he came up to my mother and said, 'Mr Laurel and Mr Hardy would be pleased to see your son now, madam.' Suddenly daunted by the prospect and without my mother, I followed him up the aisle and backstage to the entrance of the star dressing room. 'Go on, then. Knock on the door,' he said. I gave it a nervous tap and, seconds later, it swung open. There were my idols taking off their make-up.

'Ah, hullo,' said Stan, 'I hear you've come for a spot of tea. Do you like cream buns by any chance? Olly, what have you done with them?'

'I've no idea,' said Olly, 'but I know I left two somewhere for the boy.' He then rose from his chair, upon which, squashed completely flat, since he was not exactly a light man, were the crushed remains of two cream buns. 'I think', he said, 'they'll still be fit to eat.' Two more buns were ordered and brought in post-haste. Whereupon, as I ate them avidly and sipped my tea, stirred with his finger by Stan, the two proceeded to entertain me for fully half an hour.

With their make-up off, I noticed that they both looked older than I expected and Stan, in particular, seemed like a tired man. There was a slight tremour in his hands. They didn't tell jokes, they just talked nonsense and bickered as they did in the quieter moments of their films. There was no room, even in the star dressing room, for pratfalls. 'Have you heard, young man,' Stan said at one point, 'that tea, provided it is not too hot, is an excellent substitute for shampoo?' And taking a saucerful of mine he offered it to Olly who took the saucer, looked at it with the utmost contempt and deposited the contents down the back of Stan's trousers. Whereupon, of course, Stan started crying. 'Now look what a mess you've gotten me into,' he said.

'Well,' said Olly, 'you deserve it, you . . . you . . . nin-com-pip.'

They tried their darnedest to make me laugh but I was beyond laughter in the sheer wonder at being in such close proximity to two of the greatest clowns in cinema history. I hope they had some inkling that it was the highpoint of my life to date, and I have to say that it has certainly remained one of them ever since. Their kindness to a small boy, who was apparently the only one who had requested to see them, was quite extraordinarily generous. They adhered absolutely to their stage and screen personas, with Stan in tears again when he saw that Olly had sat on the buns, and Olly complaining that Stan had put them there, picking them up with that amazing, almost feminine precision that he used to employ when trying to prove that even a fat man could be gentility itself.

At the end of the half-hour they called for my mother, who was by that time pacing about outside. Both kissed her and bade me goodbye. 'You've got a very good-looking mother,' Stan said as he shook my hand. 'I've no doubt you'll turn out all right one day yourself.' I wandered away in a dream, and so, I think, did my mother. They were not exactly Ivor Novello. But as far as I was concerned, they were the better substitute.

My mother's saving graces were her warmth, charm and, especially, her sense of humour. She was a good mimic, capable of peals of laughter when confronting the more absurd facets of life in Bexhill, once described as a small town full of small people. And when she made up her mind, her charm could be devastating and the men she knew all seemed slightly or wholly in love with her. Which she liked, even when she didn't much care for them.

But, for all that, she seemed largely to have given up on life. When she sighed, and she often did, it seemed as if she were expressing years of disappointment and frustration. We got on well enough, sharing the same sense of humour, but the intimacy and the laughter had their limits. We revealed to each other almost nothing about ourselves. But I knew that the marriage was a disaster. I asked myself (but never her) why they remained living together and guessed it was that she had nowhere to go, and no money either. She contented herself with saying, when riled, that she stayed with my father because of me and that I should be grateful. But that was only after the regular rows, which were usually about her running up a bill somewhere or other. There was always a shouting match if she had left the boiler on too long for the hot water. When she did, it began to make a cracking noise that sounded particularly ominous. My nightmare was that one day it would explode and set fire to the whole place. My father's nightmare was that the bill would be huge. That cracking noise has remained with me all my life as some kind of prelude to disaster. To this day, I can't hear the noise of water in the pipes without a momentary flash of that fear.

The near disaster I remember best was when my mother fell asleep in her nightdress near an electric fire that had not been turned off by my father, and awoke to find herself in flames. She staggered downstairs and into the bedroom where I was already half asleep. It was like a scene from Dante's *Inferno*. I quickly wetted a towel in the basin and threw it over her. Amazingly, she only suffered superficial burns. But the horrendous vision of her blazing arrival in the darkened room haunts me still.

Our relationship was close but her comforting warmth and love tended to be turned on and off like a tap. There was always this feeling that I was just one compartment in her life and that she did not want me to interfere with the rest of it.

My mother had various female friends whom my father avoided as far as possible. When they came in to visit, he went out. There were a great many flirtations. I recall a stuttering late-middle-aged tutor who was brought in (as a friend) to get me through School Certificate French with a credit (he did). Anyone could see he adored her. She couldn't possibly have found him attractive. What she liked was the admiration. When Mr Pilcher arrived to give me a lesson, she was careful to spend more time than usual on her make-up. Nothing whatever happened, since Mr Pilcher, a bachelor, was terminally shy and could hardly get a word out when he came face to face with her.

60

Another 'affair' took place with a tall, thin and equally unprepossessing gentleman, already married, called Robbie. He lived at Channel View too and treated my mother as some kind of goddess fallen on hard times. In his case there was an extraordinary culmination to the flirtation. My mother would lie in her bed at night without taking off her make-up, so that Robbie could peer through the bedroom window at her from the pathway that led along the back of the twelve houses that formed Channel View. He did so regularly, without ever saying a word, until one night the police were alerted by a neighbour and he was dragged him off to the station for questioning. My mother had to say that he was a friend of hers searching for his lost cat, whereupon the police gave up attempting to prove he was a some kind of Peeping Tom. Thereafter all contact ceased.

My mother was terminally bored at Bexhill. Even the unprepossessing Pilcher and Robbie were better than nothing. She needed human admiration wherever it came from. She listened to the radio, read magazines, went to the cinema occasionally and to the local repertory company's shows more regularly. But she seldom buried herself in a book. Nor did she seem to have much depth of interest in any of the arts. If she considered my father to be hopelessly anti-intellectual, she did little to persuade me that she held the key to all that was missing in him. She lived life in Bexhill in total stasis, as if there were no way she could engage with either the present or the future beyond fortune-telling with her friends.

Horoscopes were her hobby. There were those who were psychic and those who were not, she said. And those who were could foretell the future any way they liked. There were tea leaves, cards, star signs and birth dates. She studied them all, but I don't remember any seances. I regarded the whole business as gobbledegook, but couldn't help wondering what my horoscope foretold. One psychic friend of hers studied mine and wrote a long treatise outlining my character and future. It suggested that, after early disappointments, I would eventually succeed at 'some sort of writing' – an accurate enough description of a critic. I would also become 'fairly well-known, particularly in London'. I clung on to this, more in hope than expectation, for a good many years. Being Catholic, my aunt Phyllis decried hocus-pocus but still consented to have her own horoscope done. My father refused. 'I'm playing golf with Colonel Wrixon-Harris today,' he once said to me. 'Ask your mother what the tea leaves foretell!'

Early one morning, long before we were up, Manners and family decamped, never to be seen again. Much of the silver went with them. I could never discover exactly what precipitated the exodus. I only remember there was no breakfast that morning and my father came upstairs from the dining room to announce that the table wasn't laid and 'the buggers have gone'.

This was the post-war period when people had better things to do than servanting for the sake of a room, full board and a small wage. My bet is that the Manners family simply had enough, or perhaps had received a rather better offer elsewhere. Rita, their daughter, was the only one I missed, and I rather wished I'd done something about her. I did grab her once when she brought in the tea and my parents were out. But she told her mother who told my mother who explained that Rita was not the girl for me. This was because she was 'common' – a word that was routinely used to describe almost everybody at Bexhill. 'Nice, but a little common, don't you think?' they used to say about all the girlfriends with whom I associated. This meant that their accents were not quite right, nor their dress sense. It wasn't simply a matter of a heavy regional accent, but usually a slight mispronunciation of the 'ou' in words such as house or the 'ow' in down. Anyone who said 'heouse' or 'deouwn' or 'abeout' was 'common'.

There was a suburb of Bexhill-on-Sea, where I grew up, called Little Common to which my mother used to refer as Thoroughly Common. But, joking apart, you didn't say 'pardon?' when a simple and direct 'what?' would do. You didn't say 'mirror' when 'looking glass' would do, and you certainly didn't say 'lounge' when 'sitting room' was meant, especially if you had the temerity to pronounce it 'leounge'. Edward Heath, during his time as Prime Minister, was ridiculed even in his day for this kind of speaking, especially when he referred to his yacht as '*Morning Cleoud*'.

I once queried all this with my parents, complaining that it would be rather ridiculous to recite, 'Looking glass, looking glass on the wall, who is the fairest of us all . . . Thou wert, O Queen, but now I am, I wean' . . . My father saw the point, but not my mother who replied, 'You can say deown and eout and reound if you like. But I shall stick to down and out and round!'

Once my mother heard someone walking along the Promenade saying 'Pardon?'. 'Don't say pardon, say what!' she bellowed from the veranda. It wasn't apparently 'us-you-we' to use the strange phrase she sometimes used. She invariable regarded the few friends whom I gingerly introduced to her as 'quite nice, but rather common' except for a young girl with a double-barrelled name and no chest who she thought might be right for me. Her name was Pamela, and I didn't like her very much. When I told my mother so, she opined that I was beginning to talk common myself in the effort to ingratiate myself with the girls I fancied.

At one point, she did a rather strange thing. She asked me to kiss her full on the lips as if I were snogging with a girlfriend. I objected at first but eventually did what I was told. 'Yes,' she said, 'that's not at all bad. I don't think you'll exactly be a ladykiller. But you won't lack women in your life.'

Long after I knew all about the birds and the bees, my father attempted to tell me the facts of life. I told him quickly not to bother. I felt I knew as much as he did, which might not have been too much. I'd picked up quite a lot of it from Marie Stopes's famous *Radiant Motherhood*, which I discovered in my mother's bedroom one day. This book, intended partly to explain to women that sex was not just for the pleasure of man, was the nearest one could get to erotic literature in the Bexhill of the time, and I noticed that some of the most daring bits had been underlined in pencil. Even so, I felt its main lessons had probably passed both my parents by. The only advice my father ever gave me about women, perhaps

Etienne Bellenger at the East Sussex Hunt.

reflecting on his own experience, was that it was almost certainly better to marry for something other than love or lust. 'It's amazing', he said, 'how fond one can get of a woman with money.'

My parents still had some rich friends, one of whom was a Frenchman who worked for a prominent jewellery firm and drove one of those lovely old Citroëns that would suddenly rise off the ground when you pressed a button. This seemed very grand to us. But Etienne and Madeleine were not so much grand as moneyed. Etienne liked food and sex, in that order, and would take us out to lunch or dinner at the kind of expensive places we would never have visited ourselves. When the bill arrived, my father would struggle long enough to find his wallet so that he could allow Etienne sufficient time to offer to pay himself. Champagne was followed by expensive wine and then by brandy, and the food was usually lobster or oysters. Then there were the Cuban cigars, which my father grabbed with some alacrity, forsaking his pipe. Etienne would, during these lunches, persist in telling rude stories about the sexual quirks of his friends, and Madeleine, who was well aware of his various mistresses, would bridle with simulated shock. She was a plain woman and knew it, and there were no children. God knows what she'd been through with her husband. 'Oh, Etienne, please,' she would say. 'Not in front of the boy.' My father was wont to chuckle to himself but tried to preserve the impression that he didn't hear. My mother laughed out loud. The only joke I remember vividly was the one about Cuban cigars which, Etienne said, were so good partly because they were rolled on the thighs of beautiful Cuban virgins. He told us that a friend of his had once sniffed the cigar he offered him and remarked, 'A little too near the arse, I think.'

It was a very odd friendship, more to do with Etienne's apparent affection for my father, whom he had known for many years, than my parents' fondness for him. But when he announced he was coming down to Bexhill we all prepared for something special – at least to eat and drink. I used to regard the invitations with less pleasure than my parents since Etienne would occasionally ask me embarrassing questions like: 'Derek, have you had a woman yet?'. Whereupon even my mother would say, 'Please, Etienne!' and Madeleine would tell me to take no notice of him. Then one day, he said to my parents, in front of me and much to Madeleine's horror, 'I will take him up to London and give him a taste of ze flesh – you will like it, Derek, eh?' By that time I wished I were under the restaurant table where nobody could see me blushing.

Though Etienne and Madeleine hardly qualified, being French, the world was divided by my parents not into men and women but into ladies and gentlemen, and the rest. The 'rest' should be treated nicely, but you couldn't get too familiar because they'd only take advantage. There were some exceptions to the rule. My father used to play golf with a dentist called Quinton – 'He's Jewish, you know, and hardly a gentleman. But quite a decent sort all the same.' Actually, Quinton did my teeth at his surgery in St Leonards, and invariably hurt me and made my gums bleed. I travelled there on the tram with a sense of increasing dread but, years later, another dentist told me that whoever had dealt with my mouth had done an extremely good job, Jew or not, as my father might have said.

By now, home help was at a premium. But a Mrs Holdsworth was found, separated from her husband, with another rather attractive daughter to look after. She stayed loyally with the family for some years. What Mrs Holdsworth thought of us I never knew until many years later when I mentioned her in a piece I wrote for the *Guardian* about my youth at Bexhill. I got a surprisingly warm letter from her enquiring about my parents and remembering them more fondly than they probably deserved, considering they would often complain that she kept the cream on top of the milk for her daughter rather than for my parents' porridge. I think she must have got used to the oddity of the Malcolm household where my father did the morning's shopping, except on hunting days, while my mother lay in bed until lunchtime unless lured out by one of her friends for mid-morning coffee.

When I came home for the school holidays, I still slept on the living-room sofa, since Mrs H and daughter slept in what was once my bedroom. I occupied myself during the day either going to the cinema (there were then three in Bexhill, and the programmes changed twice a week) or travelling by train to watch Sussex play cricket at Hove, Eastbourne or Hastings. At the cricket, I met a Mrs Ticehurst who became a sort of surrogate aunt. She kept a deckchair ready for me in the members enclosure and even gave me some of her sandwiches at the lunch interval. She was a tough lady who watched Sussex, not then one of the top teams, with the same sort of despairing hope that I did and went home as depressed as I did when they once again failed to shine. On one unforgettable occasion she rose from her deckchair, with surprising alacrity considering her age, and caught a ball whacked for six by Hugh Bartlett, the hard-hitting Sussex captain. There were cheers all round the ground.

In the winter it was football and Brighton and Hove Albion at the Goldstone Ground. Mrs Ticehurst never ventured there, since cricket was the only sport in which she took any interest. The truth was that I got out of the house as often as I could during the school holidays and took the train to Brighton, Eastbourne or Hastings with some relief. It was too depressing to be sitting around at 2 Channel View for long, unless my mother was in one of her more cheerful moods or my father decided to take me on the tram to the nearby golf course at Cooden Beach. He went round alone while I tried in vain to conquer the specially designed putting course and surreptitiously smoked De Reske Minor cigarettes.

CHAPTER 3

DOODLEBUGS AND DECAY

By the time I was packed off to Eton at the age of twelve, I could never decide whether it was better to be at school, which I hated, or at home, where the equilibrium was so perilous. Home grew worse and worse as my schooldays progressed. Mrs Holdsworth finally left us and no further servants, as my mother invariably called them, could be found. The house grew dirtier and dirtier and shabbier and shabbier. The small garden leading on to the Promenade became overgrown with weeds, the wooden balcony, from which my father and I used to watch the German Doodlebugs during the war (pilotless German planes full of explosives whose engines cut out before they floated down to do their damage), was in a state of near collapse, paint peeled everywhere and the inside of the house at Channel View began to look like a battlefield through which my mother and father made their way, seemingly unaware that the place hadn't been cleaned or tidied for months. There was also very little food in the larder that hadn't gone off.

Our saviour on occasions, generally during

school holidays, was Aunt Phyllis, my mother's spinster sister who had become a Catholic convert in her teens. She once took me to church to kiss the hand of a passing bishop, telling me that all my sins, up to that point, would be instantly forgiven. What, I thought, even the self-abuse? I think she would have liked me to convert too but hastily I always changed the subject. For one thing, all that incense made me sneeze, and I would have missed my father taking me to St Barnabas C of E services, at which, to amuse me when the sermons got boring, he would attempt to hang his umbrella or walking stick on the hat of any unfortunate woman who was seated in the row in front of us. 'You'll keep your father under control next time, I hope,' the vicar said as I left the church one Sunday.

Though only slightly younger than my mother, Aunt Phyllis was a different animal altogether. She was small, plain, shabbily dressed, and had the nervous habit of clearing her throat at least twice a minute. When she spoke it was often with a strange little girl's voice that seemed to beg for pity or at least some understanding of the difficulties she faced in life, especially with her health, which was never good. She was so often about to see the doctor and so often told that the cure to whatever ailed her was an operation that I felt she could not possibly live as long as she actually did. 'I'll be having my operation soon,' she used to tell me. 'They say it's very dangerous.' She seemed to survive these traumas bravely enough but complained of 'adhesions' that caused her constant pain. It may partly have been just a cry for love, because she always seemed to be alone. She had never married, had thought about becoming a nun but had gone into teaching instead. She was forever trying to pass exams on elocution, singing, piano playing and even dancing. None of these proved easy since her talent was strictly limited. But, if determination had received marks, she would have passed everything with flying colours. She wanted to qualify as a private teacher, and she began to speak with the kind of clipped accent elocution often seems to encourage in those who take the lessons. She regarded herself as a second mother to me and I had cause to be duly grateful. She was critical of my real mother and sympathised with my father, who she felt was not being looked after properly and deserved better.

She had lived for a spell in a downstairs flat at the opposite end of Channel View but gave it up in the end for a caravan somewhere in Kent, where she was less at the beck and call of my parents. I visited her once or twice but the caravan, of which she was inordinately proud, wasn't much to my taste. At the end of term, she would come down to rescue me from the shambles at 2 Channel View, generally at the summons of my mother and with the promise of a small weekly fee from my father. She slept in the bedroom now vacated by the servants and cleaned the house as best she could, cooked the meals, did the washing and generally acted as my parents' skivvy. She tried her hardest to look after me, telling me that my mother was hopeless at anything practical and had never been a good support to my father, whom she seemed to admire more than he did her. They both took her completely for granted, though relying on her utterly while she was around. Aunt Phyllis slaved away not exactly with good grace but perhaps taking small pleasure in being with what passed for a family, rather than on her own. When she returned to her caravan, however, she did so with some relief. She was worn out. I grew genuinely fond of her since I had no doubt what would have happened to me had she not been there to save the day. For a start I would hardly have eaten.

She was so different from my mother that I couldn't imagine how the two women were related. Without her, life was now virtually intolerable at home. It wasn't the rows – there were fewer of those as age took its toll. It was the shambles that depressed me. It was almost impossible to use the bathroom because of the filth, since nobody bothered to clean the bath or the wash-basin, and the grime grew thicker and thicker. The lavatory was worse. Spiders' webs hung from the corners of the rooms. There was dust everywhere. The furniture, which included some fine antiques, was gradually falling apart, and the kitchen was generally piled with dirty plates and half-eaten food.

Dorothy Malcolm at 2 Channel View.

Dorothy Malcolm, still handsome at 65.

The post-war world hit my parents hard. A way of life (and an income) which had been tenable before the war simply wasn't possible after it. My father was reduced to having bread and milk for supper, washed down with a whisky and soda. My mother would content herself with a boiled egg and a piece of toast, supplemented by a cup of tea, drunk delicately from a once grand but now chipped and stained china cup. Lunch was a forgotten meal unless Aunt Phyllis was around. When she wasn't (and she came less and less towards the end of my school life) 2 Channel View became a virtual slum.

It was inevitable that my parents would have to leave and take a smaller flat, though how they would manage even that seemed problematic. By now they went their own ways, hardly speaking to each other. My father still hunted, played golf, went to bridge at his club and read. He became slightly more ambitious in his shopping when I came home. But there was no one to cook what he bought except when Aunt Phyllis was there. In her absence, my mother made the occasional attempt but with no very edible results.

She spent much of her day in bed. Cornflakes, toast and eggs were my staple diet. The food at Eton was bad enough, except for the rhubarb crumble. But at home it was a good deal worse. There were no visitors any more. I wouldn't have dared invite any of my few Bexhill friends in, especially girlfriends. Occasionally I went out to see them at their generally immaculate suburban houses, envying the order everything seemed to be in. When I crept back home, I wondered how two people could possibly live like this without confronting what a dismal existence they shared.

The effect on me was long-lasting and profound. It was as if the world in which I lived was gradually disintegrating around me, but nobody else who lived in it even noticed. I've had a horror of squalor ever since, and every time I see a row of those tidy suburban houses with neat gardens some people like to despise, I feel a peculiar glow of comfort. Here at least everything *seems* right with the world.

Each year when the Wimbledon tennis came round, I was invited to stay at my aunt Lena's. She was the well-off widow of one of my father's brothers. During the second week of the tournament I was given my aunt's inherited debenture tickets for either the Centre Court or Court No. 1.

My aunt's prosperous if lonely lifestyle was a

Douglas Malcolm (second from right) at regimental reunion.

world away from 2 Channel View. Her large suburban residence was well looked after by her butler-cum-chauffeur, Maggs, and his housekeeper wife. Maggs used to drive me to the tennis in the Bentley, equipped with a packed lunch courtesy of Mrs Maggs. And he'd fetch me at the main entrance at the end of the day's play. I managed to see almost every final from 1947 to 1956 that way and thereafter, when my aunt died and the debenture tickets were no longer available, I found it difficult to queue up for spare standing Centre Court tickets. And where was the Bentley to fetch me at close of play?

'You'd better go,' my father used to say, 'She might leave something to you in her will. She'd better leave something to me because I gave her £5000 once.' And she did leave something to me: £1000, which came in exceedingly useful during my university days. But she left not a penny to my father. When he heard the news, my mother told me that he went straight to the beach, sat down and covered his face with his hands. I was away in Cheltenham at the time and my mother, showing far more affection for my father than I thought possible, sent me the following letter:

Derek Darling,
Daddy's had the bad news today – that Lena has not left him a penny and he is very upset at not being thought of at all – he just can't get over it – poor old boy I do feel sorry for him as he could so well do with it

– it's a bitter blow! Money always seems to go to money and those who will get it are already so well off . . . I hate to see him upset, he is getting so old-looking and it would have cheered him up – such is life!

Fondest love,
Mummie

I thought perhaps it was partly my fault since Aunt Lena was always enquiring what I wanted to do in life, and my replies can't have been too

Douglas Malcolm (middle) on the
golf links at Cooden Beach.

convincing as I really had no idea. But I supposed she would have liked me to go into the Army, the Civil Service or some other respectable profession and I did mention these as possibilities. Once she asked me, when we were out driving in the Bentley, whether I had 'ever considered the Church' and it was only quick thinking that made me reply that it was an idea I needed to think about carefully before coming to any decision. It was like a game of cat and mouse, during which I was determined to prove that I was just the sort of person who deserved a legacy one day, and the larger the better. To me, Aunt Lena was the rich relative who seemed to want to do something for my father, even if it was only to put his son on the straight and narrow. She was kind to me, but I was a bit scared of her.

When we used to have our little conversations in the Bentley, she would shut the glass partition between the front and back seats so that Maggs couldn't hear. He would have had a good laugh if he had, since he and Mrs Maggs understood more about me than Aunt Lena ever did, and had almost certainly picked up as much about my family's affairs as she had. An exceedingly conventional Scotswoman, she must have known what had happened all those years ago and, like so many, took my father's side. But she didn't let on to me.

As the house decayed around me, I used to rummage about in my father's bureau to see if he'd left any money around, so I could take myself off to the cinema or buy a packet of cigarettes. It was easier than asking him for it and receiving the inevitable grimace. He considered the cinema a chronic waste of time unless there was a newsreel of the Grand National on the programme, where-upon he would join me. One day, I pulled out a book hidden under some papers. It was called *The Judges and the Damned*, and subtitled 'An enthralling anthology of drama, scandal and sensation in court'. It was decidedly not the sort of book my father would read and, browsing through the chapter head-ings on the contents page, I read: 'Mr Justice McCardie tries Lieutenant Malcolm, page 33.' But there was no page 33. The chapter had been ripped out of the book. The author was Edgar Lustgarten, the criminologist, whose books were as popular as his later television introductions to dramatised cases were to become. Judging by the florid introduction, I guessed that the case was serious. It read: 'Covering a whole gamut of human drama and inhuman crime, Mr Lustgarten recreates, with his own un-rivalled forensic knowledge and literary skill, the impress of a judicial personality, the cut and thrust of great advocacy, the revelations of minds and motives – all the elements that can hold the court-room in a spell as binding as that of any theatre.'

The book had been removed from Bexhill Library and was well overdue. I couldn't find another copy of it there, and in the end had to order one from a local bookshop, making sure that I picked up the post every morning before my parents. When it came, I locked myself in the lavatory, sat down on the seat and read the relevant chapter. It began:

> Everyone wanted the prisoner to get off. The privileged and breathless company in court, gripping their precious seats from a subconscious fear of losing them; the unlucky and disappointed throng outside, unable to tear themselves away, the unseen multitude from the length and breadth of Britain devouring each edition of the papers, and then waiting in mingled hope and apprehension for the next – one and all devoutly wished Lieutenant Malcolm to go free. Even that granite prosecutor, Richard Muir, whose thankless task it was to present this murder charge, momentarily disclosed the trend of his own feelings when he warned the jury: 'Beware of sympathy.' For what exactly had he done, that stalwart fighting soldier, to be snatched from the peril of death in the Flanders trenches and placed under the selfsame peril in the Old Bailey Dock?

The prose was so purple that I could hardly bear to read on. But, by the time I came to the end of the chapter, I knew why my father had torn it out of the book. At Bexhill, he had finally escaped the notoriety the case had engendered until the Lustgarten book threatened to blow his cover. He had shot my mother's lover on returning from active duty during the First World War.

It was pure, Victorian-style melodrama. Just as most children can't imagine their parents making love, I couldn't conceive of a time when mine were in love at all – let alone that a murder would result from their marriage.

I suppose the discovery should have been a profound shock to me, but I don't remember it that way. I was annoyed mainly that Lustgarten had written in such lurid, tabloid terms about my father's case and scared that my father would find out that I now knew his secret. I also wondered if my mother knew of the Lustgarten book but assumed, since I'd seldom seen her read, that she had not.

It struck me that the whole affair explained much about my parents' tortured relationship and that both of them had acted with extraordinary foolishness. The last thing I did was to blame my father, who was clearly besotted with my mother at the time. I felt he was hardly responsible for what he did. When I carefully put the book back in its place and left the room, I took myself off to the cinema to a Roy Rogers film. The trick seemed to work. That night I went to bed and, surprisingly perhaps, thought very little about my discovery. But I resolved to tell no one, not even Aunt Phyllis, whose perpetual hints at dark secrets in the Malcolm household's past finally seemed understandable.

It was only half a century later, poring over columns of old newsprint, that I was able to piece the story together. And the more I did, the more curious I became.

PART II

Douglas Malcolm.

CHAPTER 4

THE INQUEST

20 August, 1917

The first witness at the packed Paddington inquest into the death of Anton Baumberg was the woman my mother called Bunny. Mrs Violet Brett was a respectable middle-aged widow who lived in Knightsbridge Mansions. They had been friends for some time. If, like the reporters and onlookers at the time, we follow the story through the evidence as it was given then, the coroner began by taking Bunny back to the start of the affair, earlier that summer.

Bunny had been persuaded unwisely to allow my mother and Baumberg to stay together at her cottage in Hampshire while my father was away in France. She must have known what was going on between the two, believing herself to be a woman of the world. She was, however, obviously worried that my father might find out. She did not want to be blamed for encouraging an illicit romance. But, on the fringes of the fashionable London society within which my mother moved so confidently, she also did not want to be considered either illiberal or censorious. The inquest and the subsequent court case placed her into a very awkward position.

Like everyone else, she had no idea that my father was back on leave and had returned to London in search of his wife, nor that a servant would tell him the address of the country cottage. This led her deeper and deeper into the whole affair, and made it virtually impossible for her to avoid seeming like the person responsible for encouraging the fatal liaison.

Fatal charm . . . Count de Borch,
real name Anton Baumberg.

As for my father, the speed at which he reached the cottage in search of my mother suggested he had more than an inkling that something might be wrong, and the way he burst into the cottage confirms it. Did he know of Baumberg's friendship with my mother? We must assume that he guessed they were having an affair. But, as an intensely jealous man who felt himself an outsider in my mother's society circle, he might well have been suspicious. He might well have been worried that she would eventually be attracted to someone else – to someone who seemed more suitable than the well-off but not very sophisticated Scottish gentleman she had married.

Bunny told the coroner that she had met my father in the hallway of her cottage and that he had asked where my mother was. He was carrying a riding crop. She had said hastily she would fetch her for him, but he had brushed roughly past her and rushed up the stairs, calling 'Dorothy . . . Dorothy.'

'The next thing I heard', she said, 'was Mrs Malcolm saying loudly, "Vi, Douglas is killing Anthony." I ran upstairs and said to Mr Malcolm, "It is stupid of you to act in this way. Nothing wrong has happened." Then I went into Baumberg's room and found him lying, clearly stunned, near the window. Mr and Mrs Malcolm had by then left that room and gone to Mrs Malcolm's bedroom. They were there for two and a half hours but I have no idea what occurred between them.' She assumed they were arguing with one another about the presence of Baumberg, exacerbated by the fact that he was not fully dressed. She added, in answer to the coroner, that

Mrs Malcolm and Baumberg were 'very friendly together', though on one occasion there was 'a slight quarrel' between them about the fact that Baumberg was living with a German woman. It upset Mrs Malcolm, she said, who was clearly jealous.

According to Bunny, later that day the Malcolms left for London together but Baumberg had stayed on to recover from his injuries. And, back in London, Baumberg had turned up at her London home with a gun which, he said, was 'to protect himself from further assault'. He had shown it both to her and Mrs Malcolm, who was staying with her at the time, and it was definitely loaded.

It was, however, my mother rather than Bunny Brett whom the assembled throng who crowded the coroner's court had come to see. She was described in the *Daily Mirror* as heavily veiled, tall and beautiful with dark, flashing eyes. Her evidence was surprisingly frank despite the fact that she must have known that her liaison with Baumberg would hardly make her popular with either the press or the public. Under the circumstances it was also rather brave. Curiously, my father did not attend the inquest either as a witness or as an observer. He was, however, represented by a solicitor called Roome, a junior partner of Sir John Simon, who was to defend my father at the trial.

My mother said she had met Baumberg on 1 April at a tea party. He had asked permission to call on her, though he knew she was married. She had accepted and thereafter he paid frequent visits. He had admitted to her that he had no real title. The name de Borch was, in fact, his father's. But the fact that his mother was an orthodox Jew meant that he could not, according to his mother's faith, take it legally. He was half Russian and half Polish, and had managed to get into England from Berlin at the outbreak of war, because 'he feared being shot as an English spy' if he stayed. Not very cleverly, he had left his passport behind with some of his baggage at Berlin railway station.

The coroner then handed her a letter she had written to Baumberg, before the Hampshire visit, which read, 'My husband has returned, and so I shall not be in tonight. I shall let you know when I shall be able to see you again, but I fear not for some time. Yours sincerely, Dorothy Malcolm.' Judging by the formal signature, the affair had not yet begun.

My mother admitted that she had seen Baumberg at her flat later and 'also at other places'. Shortly before 14 July, she was a guest at Mrs Brett's cottage. Baumberg was also there.

'Did you know your husband was coming home on leave at that time?' the coroner asked.

'No, it was about midday and I was in the Count's bedroom.'

'Who was present?'

'The Count.'

Asked what happened then, my mother replied,

'I heard my husband call from halfway up the stairs. He pushed the door wide open and came in. There was a frightful scene, as my husband heatedly objected to the Count's presence there.'

Dorothy Malcolm.

'What did he say?'

'He didn't say much at all, but struck the Count with his fists on the forehead.'

'Did the deceased strike back?'

'No, he fell down. There was a sort of scuffle beforehand. The Count put his head down and his hands up to ward off the blows. When he fell down, he seemed to faint.'

'When he was down, did your husband do anything else to him?'

'I cannot remember. Mrs Brett, our hostess and friend, came up just after.'

'Had your husband said anything to you before this scuffle?'

'No.'

'Did you ever mention Baumberg to your husband in correspondence?'

'Yes, several times.'

'Mentioned him as an ordinary friend?'

'Yes, as an ordinary friend.'

'You made no disclosures of your feeling towards the deceased?'

'No.'

My mother added that, after the affray, she went into her own bedroom followed by her husband, still carrying his whip. There, she 'implored him to divorce me'.

The coroner: 'Did you then tell him that there had been intimate relations between you and the Count?'

'Yes, I did.'

'Did he believe you?'

'Yes. But he said he could not possibly divorce me. He has always been a loving husband. But he would not divorce me in spite of what I said.'

'Did he try vehemently and fervently to persuade you to give up the deceased?'

'Yes. But I told him I would not.'

The coroner then read a letter dated 15 July from my father to Baumberg:

To the Count de Borch

You refused to fight. All right. I challenge you to a duel – pistols or swords. You can take your choice. Tell me where you want to meet me as soon as possible. Seconds will be a difficulty for me. But I will get one.

Douglas Malcolm

My mother then gave evidence that this letter referred to the scene she had just described, and that she subsequently went with her husband to her mother's house in Hertfordshire at his request. There, he and her mother tried to persuade her to give Baumberg up, but she refused, saying again she loved him and wanted a divorce.

In answer to further questions from the coroner, she described her husband 'as a man who used to get quickly excited'. She had been three years married but had no children. Her husband was a 'man of good means' but she did not know the exact amount of his wealth or if he was rich enough to pay supertax. He was a jute merchant from Scotland, carrying on business in London before volunteering for the war. The position between them now was this – she wanted her husband to divorce her. He wanted her to give up the Count. In the end, she added, she was forced to promise her husband and her mother that she would try to do so, if he refused to give her a divorce.

The coroner then read a letter written by my mother to Baumberg:

Wolfheart,

I have just a few minutes to write. I was so happy to receive your letter and to know that you are well and, of course, hearing from you comforts me a little. D. has written to you, and if the dreadful duel comes off, I think I shall die. Wolf, write to me and seal your letters to Piper, the maid, and give my love to Bunny and tell her I have not a moment as D. never leaves me or I would write to her. I am so sorry to have let her in for a horrible scene . . . I am half dazed . . . I cannot write all that is in my heart . . .

my love to my Wolf,
Squee

Squee, she explained to the coroner, was the pet name given her by Baumberg. She identified another letter written by her husband to Baumberg which read:

Count Anthony de Borch

I have had no reply to my challenge and, in case you have not received the note written on New Milton Station I sent you by post from there – I again challenge you and leave the choice of weapons to you. You will see it is better that this should happen in France. Therefore, I earnestly hope you will arrange to get to France as early as possible. I enclose my French address.

A second letter was then produced from my mother to Baumberg:

Wolf,
   D. has gone to the War Office to try to get an extension of leave, and so I am alone and able to write to you. I am thinking of you always. Let me know you news. He has written to you again about this wretched duel. What are you going to do about it? It is awful, this uncertainty. When are you coming up to town? I hope soon as I do not like you being alone with anyone else but me. Is it horrid of me? I have had to promise not to see you till the war is over. For my mother's sake, I will do it. Wolf, I hope you are not suffering as much as I am. Oh, I do so hope you are not. My heart is breaking so I cannot write sense or what I feel. Will this suffering never end?
   So much love,
      Squee

My mother then explained that she had written to her husband while he was away at the Front. She did not want to buoy him up with false hopes, and the tone of her letter was absolutely final. She wanted a divorce. She confessed she had seen Baumberg several times after her husband had gone, despite her promise not to do so. She was in love with him and that was that. And when her husband returned, she told him she had seen Baumberg. There was 'a scene' and it was 'absolutely decided' that she could not and would not stay with her husband. She told him she wanted to go away with Baumberg. 'I mentioned that it was contemplated that I should go with him to the Continent, and I think I spoke of the difficulty of passports. My mother said in front of my husband that it was obviously no use talking to me. Then he went off to Scotland Yard and, when he returned, claimed that he had discovered that Baumberg was a procurer. I said that I did not believe that but that, even if I did, I could not live with my husband all the same. My mind was made up.'

'Why could you not live with him?' the coroner asked.

'Because I loved this man. My husband also said that Scotland Yard suspected Baumberg was a German spy, and he kept asking me for his address. I did not believe that either. I never gave his address to my husband for fear that he would harm him.'

The coroner then read out three letters. The first was from my father to Baumberg, dated 11 August.

To Count de Borch

If I ever hear of you trying to steal or even to talk to my wife again, wherever I am I will get leave to hunt you out and give you such a thrashing that even your own mother will not know you again. I will thrash you until I have maimed you for life. This I swear before God in whom I believe and Who is my witness.

D. Malcolm

The second was also from my father saying that, in case of his death, he left all his money to Mrs Taylor of Vicarage Cottage, Hertford Heath – my mother's mother.

The third, which was found on him on the day of the shooting, but unposted, was to my mother. It read:

My very own darling Dorothy,

Dear God, there is a time for everything. Everything points to it that this creature is the most insufferable blackguard ever born. I shudder to think of it, that he ever dared even speak to you drives me mad. I simply cannot stand it any longer. I am going to thrash him until he is unrecognisable. I may shoot him if he has got a gun. I expect he has, as he is too much of a coward to stand a thrashing. If the inevitable has got to happen, of course, I may get it in the neck first. You see I am quite cool. If it happens, oh, believe me, my own little darling, my beloved soul, whom I love so absolutely, believe me, it is for you only. I swear to you that I love you more than any man has ever loved a woman before and if there is any wrong in me it is because I love you too much. You are a brave woman. You are noble, honourable and upright, with what a beautiful soul! I believe in God. I said yesterday that I did not. But I do. I do, and I thank Him from the bottom of my heart for having sent me over in time to save you from this devil incarnate. Your honour is saved. Thank God, oh, thank God.

Goodbye, which means God be with you. I love you and I shall go on loving you for eternity, for ever and ever. I know I shall meet you in the next world if the worst happens, when you will come to me with open arms and those beautiful eyes shining, and say to me, 'Douggie, I forgive.'

Yours for ever and ever, and oh so lovingly,
Your husband and very own
Douggie

According to a report in the *Daily Mirror*, the coroner's voice broke as he read this last desperate letter, which must have seemed to him like a final appeal from a loving husband to an erring wife, intimating that his own death would be preferable to her dishonour. The *Mirror* added that there was complete silence after the letter was read until Mr Roome, on behalf of my father, broke it by putting further questions to my mother. Did she realise, he asked, that Baumberg had deceived her? She replied that she did not consider that he had.

'Did he ask you to leave your husband for him?'

'We both decided together that it was the best thing to do.' She added that, although she had promised her husband not to see Baumberg again until the war was over, she had 'never actually sworn not to'.

To which Roome replied, 'You see the position. Your husband was out in France fighting for his country, and he had gone away with your promise that you abstain from seeing this man?'

'I see it,' my mother replied.

Roome then called the detective-sergeant who had been with my father while he was waiting to go before the magistrate after the shooting in London. He recalled my father's words to him were, 'Ah, well. It is all over now. I went to give him a good thrashing with the whip. I gave him one before but he is such a cur. I have done all I can to keep him away from my wife and her from him . . . Scotland Yard knows about him. I called there. You can imagine how I felt when I saw the cad who has been trying to get my wife to go away with him, and me in France helpless to defend her honour. Can you wonder what I did on the spur of the moment, when I saw the cur before me who was luring my wife to dishonour?'

Roome then referred to a case in which it was decided that serious provocation reduced the charge of murder to one of manslaughter when adultery had been discovered. He asked the coroner 'to point this out' to the jury. The coroner, however, said that he couldn't do this, and told the jury that he had no further questions to ask, if they had none before beginning his summing-up.

It emerged the police had interviewed Baumberg some time before his liaison with my mother. The police had informed the coroner that they believed Baumberg was a spy who had assumed the name Baumberg when his mother had married for a second time. Her husband had allowed his stepson to call himself Baumberg. He had served for a year in the Russian Army, after which he went first to Switzerland and then, in 1910, to England where he got a job with a firm who owned magazines. He wrote for those magazines as a foreign correspondent, starting work on 35 shillings a week but later getting 50 shillings.

The coroner went on to point out that my father had said he might shoot if he discovered that Baumberg had a gun with him but his primary aim was to 'thrash him until he was unrecognisable'. That was a crucial part of his statement, and the police had given evidence that there was a pistol case in an open drawer in Baumberg's room. The jury would have to consider whether or not Baumberg went to the drawer to get the pistol, whether my father saw it and whether or not he got his own shot in first in self-defence and 'in imminent expectation of being assaulted by a deadly weapon'. 'The husband', the coroner emphasised, was evidently under 'immediate apprehension of his wife going to the Continent with the deceased'.

Baumberg had denied to the police that he ever called himself 'count' and added, 'No one can tell me to my face that I have ever insisted upon being called by that title.' Asked whether he had been in Berlin when war broke out, he had replied, 'Just before.'

There were further questions, said the coroner, about a Baroness Baumberg and a Mrs Meyer – who turned out to be one and the same person – the woman Baumberg and my mother had quarrelled about. The Baroness, Baumberg had confessed, told him she was married to a New Yorker called Henry James Meyer and called herself Baroness 'because she had a castle in Germany'. He had lived with her briefly. The police had informed him that they had reason to suspect that Mrs Meyer was a spy for Germany and asked Baumberg, 'You have been intimately associated with a woman whom we believe to be working against this country?'

'Yes,' Baumberg had replied. 'But I had no

knowledge of any such activities and no one told me of them until you did.'

'But you knew there was something wrong with her?'

'No, I can certainly account for my own actions, but not for hers.'

'You must have been in her confidence?'

'I thought so and I believed that she was not interested in national affairs. She is Paris now, where she was born.'

The police had also told him that Baumberg was a powerfully built man of five feet eleven inches – physically more than equal to my father. But they added, 'He was, however, not in good condition, being flabby.'

The coroner also asked the jury to note the evidence given by H. St John Oliver, secretary of the Junior Conservative Club. He had said that he had seen my father at the club where Baumberg, known at the club as the Count de Borch, was a temporary member and had refused to give him Baumberg's address. When my father then suggested to him that the best thing to do might be to pay Baumberg £5000 to leave his wife alone, he had replied, 'Don't be a fool. That is exactly what he wants. He is only a blackmailer. He's known at Scotland Yard, who do not give him a good character.'

A constable called Stevens, the coroner reminded the jury, had also given evidence and said that my father had come up to him in the street and said, 'Constable, I want you to go to 3 Porchester Place. I have shot a man.'

Asked how he had managed to get in, my father had replied that he had told the girl at the door that he was Inspector Quinn, from Scotland Yard. Later, he said, 'I suppose you had better have the revolver I shot him with. Wait a minute. I will put the safety catch on for you.'

A second loaded revolver had been found in a drawer in Baumberg's lodgings. There was also, the police informed the coroner, 'a lot of correspondence from a number of women'.

These letters were never produced either at the inquest or, perhaps more surprisingly, at the ensuing trial. An enterprising reporter on the *Daily Sketch*, however, unearthed a little more than the coroner about Baumberg. He reported that the deceased had come to London some years before meeting my mother and, in the several boarding houses in which he had lived, was known invariably as Count Anthony de Borch. Some of his bags and boxes bore that title and nearly every article of luggage sported a crest.

After the war began, Baumberg had joined a cadet battalion training at St John's Wood under his titled name, but later had left the Army with his papers marked, 'Discharged for irregular enlistment'. The reporter added that he appeared to be a young man of ample means and, 'although by no means a dandy, always wore very expensive clothes of the most fashionable cut'. As well as the letters from several other women, a photo-graph of the Emperor Karl of Austria was found in his bedroom at Porchester Place, to whom Baumberg bore a strong facial resemblance. It was, said the report, doubtless the likeness to himself that induced him to keep it.

But the salient points, which were to be brought out at the trial, had been made at the inquest – Baumberg was not a gentleman, was of Jewish origin through his mother and was possibly a German spy. The likelihood was that he had gulled my mother, possibly for nefarious purposes, since the police also believed he was a procurer.

The inquest ended when, on the advice of the coroner, the jury returned a verdict of homicide, but added that it was justifiable homicide in the name of self-defence. Mr Roome then attempted to make an application for bail. Nothing, said the coroner, would have given him greater pleasure than to grant the application but, since there was no precedent in a case like this, he suggested it should be made not to him but to a judge at the High Court. He therefore deeply regretted that it was his duty to commit the prisoner for trial at the Central Criminal Court in the Old Bailey.

So the proceedings ended, with Baumberg's char-acter effectively blackened, but with my mother's love for him and her own view of what happened emphasised in court for the first and last time. She had admitted the affair, asked my father for a divorce and tried to persuade him to let her leave him. Despite this, my father was clearly determined to rid her of her lover, both to preserve his own honour as a husband and to save her from a man he thought was a double-dyed villain. It must have been obvious to him that the marriage could never be quite the same again. But he might have thought that anything was better than a much publicised and probably bitterly contested divorce – anathema to the respectable middle classes in those days.

His view, and that of most people at the time, was that she had simply been led astray and that he had a right to do something about it beyond merely appealing to her to give him up. His methods were decidedly eccentric. His idea of horsewhipping Baumberg and challenging him to a duel during which one or other could well have died, might have been acceptable a hundred years previously but not in 1917. But the idea captured the public's imagination, as an almost operatic melodrama with a beautiful woman at its centre and a hero and a villain on each side. Here, after all, was a war hero, back from the trenches after honourable service, who had caught his beautiful, erring wife with a blackguard, and of Jewish origin too, which in those days was almost as bad as discovering the man might have been a spy and a procurer, since anti-Semitism, although not offi-cially condoned, was rife. My mother was event-ually characterised as a weak if gorgeous little butterfly deceived by a wicked foreigner and unable to take charge of her own destiny. Even the women who crowded the Old Bailey for the trial – incongruously dressed to kill – appeared to accept this line of argument. They were heavily encouraged by the press, which felt that the coroner had done his duty by alerting the court about Baumberg after consulting the police files, but had no alternative other than to send my father to trial.

Sketch of Anton Baumberg and (below) his grave at Kensal Green Cemetery.

My mother's statement that she had indeed had intimate relations with Baumberg was completely ignored at the trial, largely because my father insisted to his defence counsel that she had not. Was this to 'save her honour' or perhaps his own dignity? Whatever the reason, Simon was to use his protestations to great effect.

On 23 August a notice appeared in the *Daily Mirror*. It was headed 'COUNT'S' FUNERAL and read,

> The funeral of Anton Baumberg, known as Count de Borch, who was shot by Lieutenant Douglas Malcolm in his bedroom at a Porchester Place boarding house, took place at Kensal Green Cemetery yesterday. The body was taken direct from the mortuary. The service, which was unattended save by three personal friends – all young men – was conducted by the cemetery chaplain. At the conclusion of the prayers by the graveside, one of the mourners threw a white rose on the coffin, which was of dark oak and inscribed 'Anton de Borch, aged 32'.
>
> The only wreath was composed of magnificent orchids, tied with purple ribbon and bearing the visiting card of Mrs Douglas Malcolm, of 59 Cadogan Square.

CHAPTER 5

DRAMATIS PERSONAE

In the weeks between inquest and trial, the newspapers never let the story die. The great court cases, after all, were the public spectacles of their day. The *Daily Sketch* would describe the 'leading figures in this great human drama':

Lieutenant Douglas Malcolm, the accused, aged 34, a Royal Artillery officer engaged at Divisional Headquarters at the front. A handsome member of a wealthy Scottish family.

Anton Baumberg, a man of mystery, who was found dead at a boarding house. Described by Lieutenant Malcolm as a 'white slave trafficker and a spy'.

Mrs Dorothy Vera Malcolm, wife of Lieutenant Malcolm. A woman of great beauty. She has confessed that whilst her husband was at the front she had become attached to 'Count de Borch', as Baumberg styled himself.

Little beyond what the *Sketch* had itself uncovered was known about the 'man of mystery'. And we have even less information about what my mother had been doing in the first years of the war; though perhaps we can speculate on the boredom and bewilderment of a young woman who, looking to marriage to give her life meaning, instead found that events almost immediately swept her husband away. She may well been vulnerable to the offer of romance.

The marriage of Dorothy Taylor to Douglas Malcolm, 23 June, 1914.

It is easier to track my father's path through three years of war. It was only a few weeks after his wedding, in early August, that he volunteered, having watched the staff at W. F. Malcolm being led willingly to the recruiting office by his oldest brother, George, already a colonel in the territorial regiment of the London Scottish. Colonel Malcolm had seen active service in the Boer War and served there with distinction. My father at first thought of volunteering for the Royal Air Corps but after a spell of training to be a pilot, opted for the Army. He decided that flying was not for him when, during a training exercise, the floor of his biplane capsized, leaving his and the pilot's legs dangling in the air out of the bottom of the plane.

In the Royal Horse Artillery, he lived a charmed life. He was attached to the 42nd East Lancashire Division who, on the outbreak of war, were sent immediately to Egypt. Their first priority was the defence of the Suez Canal but in May 1915 they were moved to Gallipoli. Regimental history lists the strength embarking at 14,224 all ranks. When the division returned to Mena in January 1916, 'its effective strength on this day was 6,669 all ranks'. In Gallipoli and Egypt, my father survived despite the fact that so many of his men were killed or wounded. He wrote home to his parents that 'it was all a terrible waste of some of the best men we had' and 'I will never forget them and I see some of their faces in my dreams'.

In the summer of 1916, he wrote an account in his personal war dairy of the second Turkish advance on the Suez Canal. He was attached to the Ayrshire Gun Battery because they were so short of officers that only four of their own were left after Gallipoli. He was pleased because it brought him to the forefront of the action since this battery was the only one remaining that had enough horses to be properly mobile. Some of the details are fascinating. He writes of being shelled remorselessly by the Turks, led by German officers, and bombed by the German planes, sometimes all night long. Heavily out-numbered but with Australian and New Zealand support, the Allies hung on regardless.

> The hail of bullets from machine guns and rifles and shrapnel was getting awfully unpleasant, and we were getting a good many casualties at the guns. It sounds like a *Daily Mail* yarn, but at one time a man who I had just been talking to was hit on my right and one of my brother officers was hit on my left. The former was killed, poor chap, but the latter only wounded and laughed about the look on my face afterwards. This sort of thing was going on all the time, so you can imagine it was a pretty tight corner. The night time was worse, but it was funny to see our Egyptian camel men burying their heads but not their bodies in the sand as if they were ostriches who think they can't be seen that way . . .
>
> Eventually, the Australians and New

Zealanders fixed bayonets one morning as soon as it was light and charged Jack Turk as they called him. It was a pleasing sight because, from where we were, we could see white flags going up everywhere – the Turks in the frontline were chucking it in. Their casualties must have been very heavy. There were hundreds of dead lying about, including our own. It was sickening to see great big Australians and New Zealanders lying dead for a lot of dirty Turks. There was a huge piece taken out of one man's stomach so you could see right inside. But I don't suppose he would want it again, poor devil . . .

Turks surrendered in their hundreds, and I saw half a dozen Australians leading in a string of 300 camels – a wondrous sight . . . one Turkish medical officer was highly delighted at being taken prisoner because, he said, he didn't get on with the Germans, who were 'rude and arrogant towards us' . . . it reminded me for all the world like a jolly good hunt after a fox across good country, picking one's ground and choosing all the cover one could get like one chooses the best place to jump a fence – keeping one's horse in hand so as to bring him in on four legs at the end of the hunt, or in this case where the Cavalry were quartered . . .

Our battery mostly consisted of miners and they behaved awfully well and were as cool as anything, being accustomed, I suppose, to explosions in mines. They cut the dead and maimed horses clear and went on with what was left and, of course, this sort of thing makes one sick. I told one driver to get the team moving and he said in his curious Scotch accent – 'I canna, I canna ... I canna drive na mair. I have only two fingers left on my right hand', and he proceeded to show me his mangled hand in quite a matter-of-fact way ...

Poor old Robert, my big horse, the great big clumsy good-natured one who pushes up against you and was always awfully affectionate, was done in. You could do anything with him from saluting a general, which means waving a sword above his ears while you are on his back, to jumping a five-barred gate while out hunting. Poor old thing, he stopped a piece of shrapnel almost as big as himself. I lost wallets, saddle and everything. But still it doesn't matter about such things. I hated to say goodbye to him. That one shell killed four men, wounded another 15 and hurt 25 horses so they had to be shot ...

Apparently the Turks are having a bad time with cholera ... they left notices on some of their abandoned camps telling us to beware – a most clean and gentle-manly thing to do. But on one camp there was a longer message – 'We have had a very hard time. Do not advance too quickly. We do not want to be caught up. We hope you enjoyed the four young ladies [meaning the four-inch howitzers they fired at us]. They are now on their way back to Bavaria. We have one of your officers with us. He is a gentleman. He dined in our mess last night. You have won, but we would have beaten you if only we had some cavalry.

George Malcolm.

My father wrote to his new wife regularly, in a very different tone, assuring her that he was 'quite safe, and very unlikely to be hit because it's pretty safe hereabouts if you take note of where the enemy artillery fire is coming from. Don't you worry your beautiful head about a thing, my darling. We will soon be together again when this damned war is over and done with.' When he left the theatre of war on leave, a family photograph shows him winning a horse race in Egypt, none the worse for wear and in a headdress that would have reminded anyone later of Lawrence of Arabia.

Meanwhile, three months into the war, his brother George's London Scottish had been the first 'Saturday Night Soldiers' to see serious action. At Messines Ridge, sent in virtually without cover to rescue beleaguered divisions of cavalry, they acquitted themselves heroically despite sustaining great losses: 760 young territorials went into Messines. Only 140 survived. Congratulations poured in to George, their severely wounded commanding officer, from such distinguished figures as Haig, Romilly and Allenby. 'While deploring the losses you have incurred, I unhesitatingly affirm that the Allied Armies in France owe to the London Scottish a place of high honour among their heroes,' wrote the cavalry commander they had saved.

For my father, to have an elder brother of such distinction meant that somehow he had to prove himself too. That he never really did was very possibly a reason for his later unhappiness about 'doing nothing worthwhile in life'. He was identified by *The Times*, at the time of his court case, as 'brother of that Colonel Malcom who led the London Scottish in their famous charge'. George was sent back to England, returned to the war a year later, but never fully recovered from his injuries. Photographed at my christening in 1932, he looked considerably older than he was and died a year later.

It was towards the end of February 1917 that my father's division embarked at Alexandria for Marseilles. Parts of his diary, produced in court, state that on Easter Monday they advanced to Tincourt, where they had their first experience of tear gas as a major offensive started at Arras, which would cost the lives of 160,000 men in exchange for an advance of a paltry 7000 yards. It was the first of the big set-piece battles which were to make 1917 the worst year of the war as far as casualties were concerned. There was a mood of sullen disillusionment at home, exacerbated by the food and coal shortages.

By the time my father came home unexpectedly on leave early in July he had, according to his diary, 'seen some terrible things'.

> No man should lose friends so easily and to so little purpose without sustaining any injury himself. But the terrible thing is that, when the man next to you goes down, you have only a feeling of intense relief that it isn't you!
>
> It is difficult to believe that all this is happening, that those in command of us

know what they are doing. Or even that the enemy is worth fighting! If it wasn't for the prospect of seeing my darling Dorothy again, I would yield to these thoughts more than I have. One has to believe in something, and it is my love that sustains me. It is far greater than any malice I bear anybody for the situation we are all in. This war is a damned mess . . . I hear some men are shooting their officers in the back because they think they are leading them towards certain death . . . I am safe, thank God. But for how long?

The war itself – the backdrop against which the drama of changing ideas about men and women was shortly to be acted out – was almost a character in the story.

Side by side with a preliminary report on my father's Old Bailey trial in *The Times* was another article headed THE STRUGGLE FOR RUSSIA in which an unnamed correspondent began, 'Thin, tense, and with a touch of the false brilliancy that constant illness often bestows, clean-shaven Kerensky faces the small, tough and bearded Korniloff. The prize is Russia . . . It is hard for an Englishman to see clearly which is Perseus and which is the Dragon. Andromeda herself can make up her mind no better than we.' The report described how, after the murder of Rasputin and the dethronement of the Tsar, Kerensky rose to prominence, proclaiming a republican state and heading the Provisonal Government. But Korniloff, with the support of the Cossacks, was bent on restoring the monarchy, and called on all Russians to resist the German invasion and its soldiers to fight rather than support the Socialism and lay down their arms. 'Upon this chaotic aggregation of men and minds which goes by the name of Russia', ended the correspondent, 'these two will bring their influence to bear, and the result will be anxiously awaited by the world at large.'

The real Russian Revolution, however, led by Lenin, was soon to take over. An empire which stretched from the Baltic to the Pacific, and whose support for Serbia had been a catalyst of the war, was in complete turmoil. Within a few weeks the Provisional Government, defeated trying to defend the Winter Palace, had been overthrown and Lenin became the effective ruler of the Russian capital, with Trotsky Commissar for Foreign Affairs. They called for an immediate end to hostilities as Kerensky fled in a car provided by the American embassy. The Allies' eastern arm had thus been totally immobilised.

On the Western Front, there seemed to be no no escape from the stalemate of trench warfare, which was so desperately expensive in human life on both sides. General Haig, now heavily criticised as the commander of the Allied forces whose methods led to the loss of hundreds of thousands of lives, was still confident that he could eventually break through the German lines. At home questions were being raised about the casualties and the fact that any success at the Front was likely to be measured in a few yards rather than miles. If the enemy was tottering, as Haig kept on saying, it was at a huge cost in Allied dead and wounded. My father had left France before the Haig offensive of late September and could thus count himself lucky, at least in one sense. The trial, however painful, was considerably less dangerous. The strange thing was that my father's case received equal publicity, as if somehow it summed up the emotional dangers of war back at home.

On the same page as the announcement of the Old Bailey proceedings, a little further down, *The Times* reported that a thirty-six-year-old London man had been sentenced to three weeks' imprisonment for stealing three pounds of sugar from a sack at the railway goods depot in Liverpool Street. He had removed the sugar with a trowel and placed it in his handkerchief. The police reported that he earned £3 to £4 weekly, and that his wife and family were practically destitute, living in two small rooms. 'How does this money go?' asked the magistrate, 'In drink?'

'No,' said the police, 'In betting.' The prisoner, *The Times* wrote, appeared dazed when his sentence was announced. Clearly he didn't have a prominent QC to represent him.

In the *Telegraph*, next to the trial report, was a

story about 450 severely wounded British soldiers arriving at Waterloo Station. There was no welcoming band and there were no cheering crowds, only motor ambulances and a small buffet cart organised by a Mrs Wilson. The paper spoke of 'this sorry proceeding' and remarked that it was by no means exceptional. The men, however, though some were badly incapacitated, remained 'remarkably cheerful throughout'.

The *Daily Mirror* reported that over 75,000 Chinese labourers had been recruited to perform menial duties behind the lines in France. They worked under contract for ten hours a day and seven days a week, and every 'coolie' had his fingerprints taken by Scotland Yard since they all looked alike to Europeans. They were less nervous under fire than the British West Indian auxiliaries but, if any were killed, refused to work until the funeral obsequies had been conducted. Those in charge of the Chinese were given a phrase book, written by a major in the British Army. The phrases included 'Less talk and more work' and 'This latrine is reserved for Europeans and is not available for Chinese'.

Alongside the *Mirror*'s preliminary report on the Old Bailey case was an announcement that a contingent of American troops would march past the King at Buckingham Palace, giving Londoners a chance to show their enthusiam for the United States' late and, in the opinion of some, belated entry into the war. A big crowd was expected to

119

line the route. By this time American troops had reached the Western Front but not in large numbers. Most of them were not fully trained and General Pershing, their commander, complained that he had a hard task at first to make a significant contribution to the hostilities.

Even in this context the trial was a front page story. The lawyers especially were the subject of popular speculation as protagonists in the drama. 'The case will be tried by Mr Justice McCardie,' the *Daily Sketch* wrote. 'Sir John Simon KC and Mr H. D. Roome will appear for the defence. Mr Richard Muir and Mr Percival Clarke will prosecute for the Crown. It is understood that Sir Edward Marshall-Hall KC and Mr J. A. C. Keeves hold watching briefs.' These men were at the top of their profession, at a time when judges and QCs were much better known to the public than they are today. Their interrogations and closing speeches were often printed at length in the papers. The final speeches, in particular, were invariably carefully prepared, honed and delivered, in the full knowledge that they would reach a wider audience than judge and jury. Frequently the subjects of hagiographical biographies that hinted at virtues a saint would envy, these men were considered to be members of an Establishment less vulnerable to mockery than today, whose opinions, even on matters other that the law, were afforded more respect than they sometimes deserved. Judges, in particular, who in contemporary times are ridiculed for not knowing who the Beatles were or thinking Beckham is a suburb of Outer London, were still regarded as the repositories of general wisdom, steeped in the classicism culled from public school.

Judge McCardie was a typical example. As George Pollock, his biographer, put it, 'Great honour in his profession, some measure of fame in the wider sphere, came to Henry Alfred McCardie not by any accident of birth, nor because his mind was forced to the fever-heat of unnatural brilliance but rather because he possessed, to a greater degree than most of his fellow men, the less picturesque but no less precious attributes of sagacity, great industry, clearness of vision and, most of all, knowledge of mankind.' McCardie remained a bachelor all his life and committed suicide by shooting himself in 1933. The son of an Irish merchant who lived in Birmingham, it was thought that he might have been gay, but the official reason for his suicide was depression after several bad bouts of flu, in those days an illness capable of killing hundreds of thousands of sufferers. He was regarded as a liberal member of the Bench – 'a man of the people,' in the words of Pollock, 'who knew, loved and understood humanity.' He was once called 'the judge with the ever-smiling eyes', but was criticised for his persistent pronouncements on social and cultural matters as much as he was praised for his learned interpretation of the law.

But McCardie was not a card-carrying liberal. In his judgment in the later case of Martial v. Frankau, which revolved around a wife's right to pledge her husband's financial credit, he said,

> Too many women are the slaves of fashion and too many men are the slaves of women . . . the ordinary society woman could clothe herself quite well for one-fifth of the money she now expends on dress. She could buy a sufficiency of stout and long-wearing woollen or flannel garments for a very small sum per annum. Cotton fabrics for the summer time are extremely cheap . . .
>
> Quite apart from the sacred trust of motherhood and the noble companionship she often gives, the function of a woman in modern society is largely utilitarian. Nature has decreed that leadership and physical strength and intellectual achievement shall belong to men, but women are the chief decorations of social life . . . women cannot be expected to renounce an essential feature of femininity or to abandon one of nature's solaces for a constant and insuperable physical handicap. A reasonable indulgence in dress is needed to counterbalance what I may call the inferiority complex of women.

In my father's case he was less Victorian in his opinions. The statement he would make during the summing-up, described as masterly by *The Times*, was brave for the time. It proposed that if a wife decided to leave her husband, on no matter how reprehensible an excuse, it was hardly the required duty of a husband to kill the man who had persuaded her to do so. And, although he almost certainly shared the same sympathy for my father felt by almost everyone else in the court, he was clearly not prepared to influence the jury overmuch in this respect. My father's case was the first highly publicised trial over which he had presided, and his first appearance of many at the Old Bailey.

Another famous figure in the case was Bernard Spilsbury, later knighted and already the best-known pathologist in the land. His task was to divine when and how the bullets that killed Baumberg struck. Spilsbury was nicknamed 'The Scalpel of Scotland Yard' and his forensic skills were considered to be second to none. He was also generally judged to be 'an incomparable witness' whose precise and lucid method of giving evidence had been noted during the celebrated Crippen case of 1910. Crippen, a fraudulent American doctor born in Michigan but living in England, poisoned his wife in London's Camden Town and buried her remains in the cellar, before being pursued by the police back to America. Prosecuted by Muir, it was Spilsbury's complicated medical evidence that effectively condemned him. Spilsbury was a leading figure in a number of notable trials and had a reputation with the public, and thus with juries, for virtual infallibility. He became a legend in his own lifetime until age and several strokes raised some doubts about methods that were eventually considered precise enough but old-fashioned.

Richard Muir, the prosecutor, was also later knighted, and made Senior Counsel to the Treasury. He worked for many years almost entirely in the criminal courts and prosecuted a number of notorious criminals, also including Dr Crippen. He eventually became a judge. Muir won the reputation of being a man who never permitted his own feelings to err on the side of mercy. But in the case of my father he was not at his most merciless. He got the brief for the Crown more or less as a matter of course, and had the feeling that the authorities were not particularly anxious for a conviction, or at least that the defendant should not suffer too harsh a penalty for his crime. When he examined his brief, it was said that Muir only decided to go through with it after a personal appeal from Sir Charles Matthews, the Director of Public Prosecutions. Muir sympathised with the defendant and his opening statement was evidence of his distaste for the task: 'It has been said many times that no motive could be adequate for murder. But in this case it would be admitted by the prosecution, and contended by the defence, that if there ever did exist or could exist a motive which would be adequate for murder, that motive existed in the prisoner on this occasion.' Muir's biographer, Sydney Felstead, records that he remarked to one of his friends, 'A verdict of murder is out of the question. Possibly the jury might bring in one of manslaughter, and even then a nominal sentence only will be imposed. I expect Lieutenant Malcolm will be bound over.'

He thought my father should have pleaded guilty to manslaughter because McCardie would then have had a chance to release him immediately on entering a surety of good behaviour. But to this Simon would not agree. Later Muir described Simon's final speech as the finest of its kind he had ever heard – which was praise indeed, considering he had been forced to listen to many of Marshall-Hall's famously eloquent and often imaginative pleas on behalf of his clients. Marshall-Hall was perhaps the most well-known QC of the day. No one knows who instructed Hall on his watching brief, but he apparently knew my mother socially, liked her and may have consented to listen to the proceedings on her behalf. It is, however, doubtful whether she could have afforded his fee, or that my father would have paid it. Possibly he was engaged by my mother's parents.

The tall and imposing Sir John Simon, defending my father, took silk only nine years after being called to the bar in 1899. As an advocate he was considered extremely able, with a complete command of the detail of his briefs and a quiet, authoritative manner that inspired confidence. Even so, he regarded the law as his second profession and as a stepping stone into politics. At the time of the case he was Liberal MP for Walthamstow and had already been a member of Lloyd George's Cabinet as Attorney-General. In 1915 he was offered the post of Lord Chancellor but refused it because he didn't want to go to the House of Lord – 'The sack,' he had said, 'rather than the Woolsack.' Instead, he went to the Home Office but resigned shortly afterwards on the issue of conscription, which he opposed, and remained out of ministerial office for some fifteen years. This enabled him to concentrate on his legal career.

As a politician he was considered more an efficient chief of staff than a bold innovator. He was never very popular in the House, largely because he was regarded as the kind of lawyer able to speak on either side of an issue with equal facility and conviction, and because he was innately shy and unforthcoming by nature. This is why many thought he was too undemonstrative an advocate for my father, but also why his cool, persuasive logic proved so effective. He was able to speak quietly with no outward show of emotion and afterwards the famously fiery Marshall-Hall, his exact opposite as an advocate, would agree with Muir that Simon's closing speech to the jury was among the greatest he had heard at the Old Bailey.

CHAPTER 6

THE TRIAL

On the first day of the case, which lasted only two days, *The Times* wrote:

The precincts of the Court were thronged almost at daybreak, and a long queue, of which but a small portion was admitted to the building, was formed outside. Most of those seeking admission were women and even when told that the Court was full, many tried door after door in the hope of securing entrance. Every available seat was occupied, the barristers' benches were overflowing, the gallery was packed, and chairs were placed round the Court wherever there was any space. So full was the Court that some of those with legitimate business were unable to get in. Mr Justice McCardie was on the bench. It is the first important criminal case that he has tried. Lieutenant Malcolm was in the dock, dressed in a dark blue civilian suit and, though he looked tired and pale, he showed great interest in the preliminary proceedings. He walked firmly to the rail of the dock and stood there with his hands behind him. When charged, he answered in low but clear tones: 'Not guilty', and sat for the rest of the day's hearing.

It is difficult to imagine what was going through my father's head as the case began. My guess is that he knew he had made a terrible mistake, a mistake which might very well ruin his life. He also knew that, although he remained deeply in love with my mother, the marriage could never be the same again, even if divorce could be avoided. Always a man with a hot and sometimes uncontrollable temper, he had, at the sight of the man who he privately knew had 'dishonoured' my mother (even though he was gallant enough publicly to insist that her liaison with Baumberg was not sexual) lost control and shot him. Now, though defended by one of the most distinguished counsels in the land and buoyed up by the knowledge that the public at large was on his side, he was said by onlookers to have possessed a fatalistic calm.

This calm was illustrated to me, albeit hilariously, many years later when, driving from Bexhill to Pevensey with me as a passenger in an old and battered Ford Popular, he lost control of the car going down Pevensey Hill on a slippery winter surface. We went round and round on the road, with my father's foot on the brakes, which made matters worse. To my surprise, my father took his hands off the wheel, took out his pipe, attempted to light it despite the fact that the Ford was totally out of control and said, as if merely passing the time of day, 'Oh, well, we're goners now.' Fortunately nothing was coming the other way and we slid to a halt at the bottom of the hill without overturning and without sustaining so much as a scratch either to the car or to us.

Waiting in the dock at the Old Bailey, he apparently seemed blessed with the same kind of cussed calm. As I knew him, he was a man who did foolish things all his life, often on the spur of the moment. But, when his actions turned out disastrously, he remained totally composed, as he was throughout the trial. He relied utterly on Simon, and, for once in his life, that judgement was completely justified.

As for my mother, the papers reported only two incidents during the course of the case. One was a half-hour visit to my father during the lunch break of the first day's hearing. Exactly what was said can only be conjectured, since I had been made to promise by my father that I would never mention the case to her. But one of her sisters later told me that she had been touched by his public insistence that she and Baumberg had not had a sexual affair despite the fact that she had told him plainly that she had. She realised that essentially he was a good man who was trying, according to his lights, to be a good husband, however much she now regretted marrying him.

She told my father that she was prepared to remain married to him whatever the outcome of the case and that, though she could never forgive him for shooting her lover, she understood that he had done so out of love for her. She seemed strangely fond of him, despite everything, and remained so for the rest of her life. But she must also have given some thought to her reputation. If she stayed with him, she would not be happy. But she would not be reviled. Besides, he could divorce her but under the circumstances it was very unlikely that she could divorce him. It seemed that there was no one around to persuade her that her beauty, acting ability and remarkable voice could have helped forge a career apart from him that might have made her financially independent.

The second incident involving my mother took place on the morning of the second day of the trial when a woman approached the court and said she wished to see my father's solicitor at once. When asked for her card, she handed the officer at the door a bulky letter, which she desired should be given to the solicitor. The officer took the letter and fetched the solicitor but, when he arrived, the woman had disappeared. The papers reported that 'the Press Association understands that the letter was from Mrs Malcolm'. No one knew what it contained, though it was possibly a written state-ment containing what she had told my father during their meeting, which she hoped might be of some use to the defence. It was clear that she did not want him to be imprisoned or worse. Even though devastated by the shooting, the possibility that Baumberg could well have been a spy and a serial seducer of women may well have begun to cloud her amorous judgement.

When the trial started and a tall, rather stern-looking Muir got up to outline the case for the prosecution, he stated the facts as if he knew the court's sympathy would be with my father. He made no attempt to attack my father's actions at Mrs Brett's Hampshire cottage and admitted that Baumberg was obviously pursuing my mother, possibly for nefarious purposes, that he had given himself a title to which he had no right and that he had taken his 'thrashing' less than manfully, being so badly knocked about that he was unable to travel back to London for several days.

His main concerns were to show nevertheless that there was no evidence whatsoever to suggest a verdict other than murder or manslaughter, 'if the facts were looked at squarely'. He was partic-ularly anxious to prevent Simon using the court's sympathy for my father to bypass the law in favour of what he called the 'unwritten law'. This unwritten law referred to cases in both France and America, where juries had often found a moral rather than legal excuse to find the accused not guilty. The case, he was anxious to maintain, was no *crime passionnel* and, even if it was, had no place in British courts.

He said that, despite the thrashing, and the two challenges to a duel to which he never replied, Baumberg had continued to see my mother. Then, Muir added, my father had written to him a third time – a letter sent to Bunny's cottage and re-directed to Baumberg's London lodgings. That letter stated that if the prisoner ever heard of him trying to see or even talk to his wife again, 'Wherever I am I will get leave and hunt you out and give you such a thrashing that even your mother will not know you again. I will thrash you until I have maimed you for life. This I swear before God in whom I believe and Who is my witness.'

My father, he went on, eventually came home on leave from the Front on 13 August and imme-diately tried to find Baumberg's London address. He asked Mr Oliver, the secretary of the Junior Conservative Club of which Baumberg, as Count de Borch, was a member. But he didn't know. When my father told Oliver what had happened, he suggested they should go together to Scotland Yard to find out if Baumberg was known to them. The Yard hadn't got his address but told them they had collected information that suggested that he was definitely an undesirable alien.

When the two left the Yard, Muir continued, my father had asked Oliver what he should now do to save his wife from the man who was attempting to seduce her. He had already given him a thrashing but that had clearly had no effect, so he wondered if Baumberg might be bought off with £5000. Oliver had replied that this was an absurd idea and probably just what 'a blackmailer like Baumberg' wanted. He suggested instead that my father should find out where he lived, take off his army uniform and go there to give him 'a second good hiding'. My father said that was exactly what he would do. Later, he saw Oliver again and showed him a hunting crop which he had purchased. He said he was definitely going after Baumberg with it, provided he could find out where he lived.

Subsequently my father did find Baumberg's address, which was at 3 Porchester Place, 'a cheap but respectable' lodging house. When he first went there he was told by a servant that Baumberg was out and would not be back until the small hours of the morning. He then went away. But, Muir said, it seemed that before going to Porchester Place, he had written a new will, cancelling the previous one that left everything to my mother, in case Baumberg got hold of the money. Instead, he left a very considerable sum to Mrs Taylor, her mother. Then he wrote a letter to my mother in which he said that he couldn't stand the whole thing any longer and was going to take the law into his own hands. He referred to Baumberg as 'the devil incarnate' and protested his undying love for his wife.

He placed the letter in his pocket and set out

again for Porchester Place. He arrived around 7.45 a.m. and was admitted by a servant. To get to Baumberg, which he otherwise might have failed to do, he told the servant that he was Inspector Quinn from Scotland Yard. She escorted him to Baumberg's room on the third floor. It was a top back room between two others. The servant then left the house for a short while – it would, said Mr Muir, have taken her a minute to get downstairs – and she heard no noise of any struggle. A Miss Knight, loding in the room next to Baumberg's, however, did. She heard my father being admitted to Baumberg's room and very shortly afterwards a 'bang'. There was then a disturbance, which caused the ornaments on her sideboard to shake.

Miss Knight heard one more loud noise, which led her to believe the bed had collapsed and, after that, some sounds that made her think the occupant of the room was tidying it up again. Finally, she heard four or five pistol shots at very short intervals. Another lodger, a Mr Pasqua, who occupied the room on the other side of Baumberg's and who was in the bathroom at the time, a floor and a half beneath, also heard some of the noise that preceded the shots, and then the shots themselves. He looked out of the bathroom and saw my father coming downstairs. My father saw him and called out, 'Don't worry. It's all right,' and continued downstairs. He was definitely carrying a hunting crop but Mr Pasqua did not spot a gun.

When my father reached the street, he saw a policeman and told him to go into the house because 'I have shot a man there'.

As the constable accompanied him inside, my father said, 'I suppose I may as well give you the pistol with which I shot him.' He produced it and added, 'I'd better put on the safety catch' before handing it over.

Baumberg was lying dead on the bed, legs dangling over the side. He was dressed in a pyjama top and nothing else. The constable telephoned for a surgeon, then took my father to the nearest police station. At the station, the new will and the letter to his wife, which had not yet been posted, were found on him. Then a Detective-Sergeant McHattie went to the house and made an examination of the contents of Baumberg's room.

Having done so, he went back to the station and said to my father, 'I have been to 3 Porchester Place and seen the dead body of Anton Baumberg. I shall charge you with wilfully murdering him by shooting him with a magazine pistol.'

My father replied, 'Very well, charge me with what you like.' The charge was then written down and formally read to him. All he said in his defence was, 'Very well. I did it for my honour.'

He was then taken to Marylebone Police Court and, while waiting to be brought before the magistrate, said to the sergeant who was on duty there, 'Ah, well, it is all over now. I went to give him a good thrashing with the whip. I gave him one before but he is such a cur. I have done all I can to keep him away from my wife and her from him. He is a White Slave trafficker and a spy. Scotland Yard knows all about him. I called there. You can imagine how I felt when I saw the cad who has been trying to get my wife to go away with him, and me in France helpless to defend her honour. Can you wonder at what I did on the spur of the moment, when I saw the cur before me who was luring my wife to dishonour?'

Continuing his recital of the facts, Muir emphasised my father's remark 'on the spur of the moment' – which did not suggest to him that self-defence was a motive, since my father had not intimated that Baumberg had attacked him. That, said Muir, was on 14 August and the prisoner was obviously still under the impression that Baumberg's 'attempts on his wife's honour' had been unsuccessful. He remained in that belief at any rate up to 20 August, because on that day he had said to the magistrate, 'May I say, sir, that a wicked and scurrilous report has appeared in the newspapers that my wife had intimate relations with this man. It is absolutely false, absolutely false. She was alone and she had no one to look after her. But it is absolutely false.'

Those were the facts, he said, on which the jury were asked to say that the prisoner was guilty of the crime of wilful murder. He had endeavoured to state them without colour or prejudice of any kind. The jury would realise that it was difficult for anyone, even if his position was advocate for the prosecution, to avoid giving the facts of this particular case a colour that was in favour not of the prosecution but of the defendant. Realising that, he also understood how much more difficult it would be for the jury to do what was undoubtedly their duty – to administer the law as it existed in England and decide on the facts in a calm and dispassionate manner. He was sure the judge would readily confirm this to them. They should on no account take notice of the 'unwritten law' he had spoken about before. England was England where there was no such thing.

Muir then directed his remarks to Simon by saying he was quite certain that no advocate, speaking in that court to an English jury, would ever ask them to do anything else. Least of all an advocate who had held high office under the Crown. In other words, Simon had better not make such an appeal. As it turned out, he did not.

And what was the law? It was, said Muir, that all homicide was presumed to be murder unless the evidence suggested otherwise. In this case, only two persons were present when the homicide was done, and one of them was dead. Even though it was possible to conjecture all sorts of things, those were the only facts that mattered. The verdict, he pointed out, might be one of three. They might find the prisoner guilty of wilful murder. They might find him guilty of manslaughter. Or they might find him not guilty if in their opinion he had killed Baumberg purely in self-defence. A man might be guilty of wilful murder even if he did not intend to kill, and even if he hoped that the act would not result in death. But if a man fired four separate shots with a pistol at close range, no one would dispute that he performed an act that would probably result in death. This was what my father did. So the law had to assume murder, and 'it rested with those who suggested otherwise to show why on earth it was not'.

Homicide might be regarded as the lesser crime of manslaughter if the person who committed the crime was forced into it by severe provocation. No provocation by words was sufficient, in Muir's opinion, to do that.

At this point, the judge intervened for the first time: 'Except, perhaps, on a sudden admission by a wife of adultery.'

Muir replied that, in his view, no provocation by words was sufficient, with the possible exception of two ways, both of which were highly doubtful. The first was threatening words, accompanied by actions showing an assault was imminent, and the second was indeed an admission of adultery. There were, however, no cases which established either in law. Besides, the second of them could not arise because it was made abundantly plain that, not only up to the date when the fatal shots were fired, but also six days later, the prisoner believed that his wife had not committed adultery. A violent assault, Muir continued, might reduce the crime of murder to manslaughter if the person attacked had tried to avoid it. But whatever the provocation, it must be bad enough to satisfy the jury that the man's judgement was totally overthrown by sudden anger and not by something which happened previously.

The jury, said Muir, had to find out two things. First, what was the state of my father's mind when he was in Baumberg's room? Did he really become so angry that he was unable to control himself? Secondly, if that was so, why did he do so? Did Baumberg assault or threaten to assault my father? The answer was surely no. The facts all pointed to calm and deliberate action on the part of the prisoner. The only statement that suggested otherwise was his statement to Sergeant Henry after the killing, 'I went to give him a good thrashing with the whip . . . you can imagine what I felt when I saw the cur who has been trying to get my wife to go away with him and me being in France helpless to defend her honour. Can you wonder at what I did on the spur of the moment when I saw the cur before me who was luring my wife to dishonour?' It was provocation of the most moving kind but it was not, in Muir's opinion, the kind which the law could recognise as proving manslaughter rather than murder.

Muir ended by saying again that there was no statement by my father that the dead man ever assaulted him, nor was there any evidence on the body of the dead man that any violence had been committed except by the bullet wounds. In other words, no 'thrashing' took place. How, then, could the jury justify the thought that the crime was other than one of wilful murder? There was neither any evidence that would justify them in reducing the crime to manslaughter nor evidence of any kind which would justify them in saying that it was homicide inflicted in self-defence.

After this speech, which the jury listened to intently, Muir called his first and only witness – Bunny Brett. He was not permitted under the law, as prosecutor for the Crown, to call my father, although he could have cross-examined him had Simon done so. According to *The Times*, Mrs Brett went into the witness box 'self-possessed enough', and readily answered Muir's less than probing questions. But when Simon cross-examined her, according to press reports, 'her calmness left her'.

Sir John opened very quietly, with long pauses between questions. He never once raised his voice. It was as if he wanted at first to bore the court to death and thus take the emotion out of the case, at least before his final summing-up. First, he tried to get out of her the admission that she knew very well about the relationship between Mrs Malcolm and the 'Count'. In this he didn't succeed but he did cause Mrs Brett to break down after ten minutes of his cross-examination. She

140

tearfully repudiated the suggestion that she had done any wrong and at one point threw the gloves she was carrying on to the ledge of the witness box and said, 'Please allow me some justice.'

She insisted that Baumberg and Mrs Malcolm had forced themselves upon her, and that she had done her best to keep them away from her flat in London. She said that when Baumberg met her and Mrs Malcolm at Waterloo Station, she had no idea that he intended to go to the country with them. Nor did she think there was anything sexual between them. She thought my mother innocent of adultery, admired her greatly for her beauty and intelligence, and said she was 'very fond of her still'.

Simon then asked her to describe the unexpected arrival of the prisoner at New Milton and the scene that followed. She said that when Lieutenant Malcolm came downstairs, she had asked him what had happened. He did not tell her but asked, 'Has this man, well, dishonoured my wife?'

She replied, 'As far as I know, no, decidedly not.'

She saw Mrs Malcolm and Baumberg again at her London flat, despite the fact that she had asked them not to come to visit her under the circumstances. There followed an exchange during which Simon once again attempted to ascertain Mrs Brett's true part in the events at her cottage that weekend.

Simon: 'Did you gather or infer before they came

to Hampshire that Baumberg was making love to Mrs Malcolm?'

'No.'

'If you had you would never have encouraged or countenanced it?'

'Certainly not!'

'When you saw Baumberg after the thrashing, was he wearing pyjamas?'

'No.'

'What was Mrs Malcolm wearing?'

'A sort of matinée coat.'

'I don't know what that is. Was she wearing a dressing gown?'

'Yes.'

'And what was the Count wearing?'

'His underwear, not his pyjamas. He was half dressed.'

'It must have been a great shock to you.'

'It was.'

'You realised it was undesirable that you should have Mrs Malcolm and Baumberg together afterwards?'

'Yes.'

Simon asked Mrs Brett, who was clearly still upset, why she had allowed Baumberg to stay in her London flat after the incident at the cottage. Mrs Brett said she had found him ensconced there and, 'He begged me not to turn him out. Out of Christian charity I allowed him to stay on.' But she admitted that, while he remained there, he was receiving letters from my mother.

'Did you know that Mrs Malcolm had promised to give Baumberg up?' Simon asked.

To which Mrs Brett replied, 'I said to the Count, what are you going to do with this lady? He replied that he loved her "very, very much". I said, "You may get her divorced, but what will you do till then?" He said, "If she will marry me after her divorce, I will marry her. I am very devoted to her."' A moment later Mrs Brett said, 'Allow me a moment please,' and then cried out through her sobs, 'These people forced their way on me. Why should you imply that I am in some way responsible for their behaviour?'

Then came Simon's final questions extracting from Mrs Brett his most important evidence if he were to establish that my father had acted in self-defence. 'While he was at your home, did Baumberg show you a pistol?'

'Yes.'

'Is this the pistol?'

'I think so.'

'Was it loaded?'

'Yes, he took the bullets out and then put them back again.'

'Did he tell you that he bought it in case Malcolm attacked him?'

'Yes.'

'Did he say that if Malcolm laid a finger on him he would use it?'

'He did.'

Mrs Brett added that it was about the time that

Baumberg received the threatening letter that he bought the pistol.

This exchange formed the basis of Simon's case for my father, since it was proved beyond doubt that Baumberg knew he was in danger and intended, if he could, to defend himself from any likely attack.

But this was still not enough for my father who held a whispered conversation with Simon after which he immediately asked Mrs Brett to be recalled. He badly wanted Simon to emphasise that Baumberg was a man who had been working against the country that had given him a home.

Simon asked her, 'On one of the occasions after Mrs Malcolm and Baumberg had met in your London flat was there a quarrel between them?'

'Yes.'

'And what was that quarrel about?'

'She asked him whether it was true that he had had a liaison with a German baroness. He admitted it and Mrs Malcolm was very upset.'

That was all Simon asked her, but he then called Mr Oliver, Secretary of the Junior Conservative Club, who confirmed that Scotland Yard had told him that the real name of the baroness was Meyer.

'She has since been caught by the French police, has she not? And shot as a spy?'

'Yes.'

Simon had made the point my father wanted. But he went further. Prompted by him, Oliver said that my father had tears in his eyes when the information about Baumberg was being revealed to them at the Yard. It was clear to him that his wife had to be saved from the man.

Simon: 'Did he say that unless he could be quick, Baumberg would be able to go off with his wife?'

'Yes.'

'From first to last was his bearing that of a man who felt that he must do his duty to defend his wife?'

'Yes, it was the manner of a gentleman.'

Oliver's remark that 'it was the manner of a gentleman' paid dividends in court, even among the few who were probably only 'nature's ladies and gentlemen'. They knew exactly what the description meant, and so did Simon who punctured the more emotional parts of his summing-up speech with words that suggested my father was a thoroughly admirable 'gentleman' whatever he had done.

The next witness Simon called was Miss Violet Piper, my mother's personal maid, who seemed to confirm that my mother was intent on going off with Baumberg. She said that there were three other servants at the flat in Cadogan Square. Mrs Malcolm had given them all notice to leave. She had bought a new trunk on which there were no initials, which arrived only on the day before my father came home.

'Did you know that she was planning to run away with Baumberg?' Simon asked.

'I knew she was giving up the flat. But the reason was not divulged to me.'

Piper was conscientiously loyal to the last, though she must have known most of what was happening, since she was the discreet conduit of the letters between my mother and Baumberg, which had to be kept secret from my father.

Simon then called Detective-Sergeant McHattie in order to underline Baumberg's villainy. On being asked to describe Baumberg, McHattie said he was about six feet tall but not an athletic man. 'He had a good chest,' he added, 'but not much of a leg. It was like a woman's – soft.' There was laughter in court at this point. Clearly he was not, despite his pretensions, much of a gentleman. Simon asked whether he could say 'something good' about Baumberg. To which McHattie replied, 'No, I cannot. He was known to be of the worst character.'

The pistol, identified by Mrs Brett as belonging to Baumberg, was then produced in court and a gunsmith was summoned. It was the same pistol that was found in a small leather case, lying on the top of some ties and letters in the drawer.

The judge asked the gunsmith whether it was possible to fire the pistol without removing it from its case. The gunsmith tried to do so in the box and succeeded. He said that if the leather case were undone, there would be no need to take the gun out in order to fire. He then explained the difference between Baumberg's pistol and the Savage used by my father. The Savage was an automatic and could fire four shots one after the other. Baumberg's pistol was of a French make uncommon in England and was only semi-automatic. The Savage recocked itself, discharged the empty shell and was ready to fire with the next pressure of the trigger finger. Baumberg's pistol needed the pressure of a hand on the grip to do the same. Simon asked whether he thought Baumberg 'would be strong enough to exert the necessary grip'. The gunsmith smiled and said he was sure of it.

Dr Spilsbury, the pathologist who made a post-mortem examination of Baumberg, described the position of the bullet wounds. Two, he said, were on the left side of the chest, one was in the neck and another almost in the middle of the forehead – the bullet which caused this wound having passed through the skull and the brain. He found it beneath the scalp. The two wounds in the chest were, in his opinion, inflicted first, followed by those in the neck and head.

Muir asked whether the witness thought the shots were fired within a second or a second and a half of each other. Dr Spilsbury said his impression was that the time must have been rather more than that – about five seconds apart. Asked the cause of death, he said shock and loss of blood.

Muir then asked at what distance the pistol was from the wound in the neck when it was fired. Spilsbury said definitely less than three feet away and possibly less than one foot.

'And from the wound in the forehead?'

'That was even closer.'

The judge then commented that he was surprised no question whatever had been asked of the police witnesses as to whether my father had any marks on his face or body that would indicate an assault upon him. This caused Detective-Sergeant McHattie to be recalled, and he confirmed what Muir had said – there were no marks on my father when he first saw him after the incident. There were, in fact, no signs of a struggle on him at all.

McHattie then explained that, at the request of Sir John, he had gone to 3 Porchester Place and, in the presence of Miss Knight, who had given evidence about the sounds she had heard on the morning of the incident, and of Sergeant Henry, he had made 'certain experiments.' He went into the bedroom Baumberg occupied, Miss Knight being in the adjoining room with the door closed. He struck the bars at the end of the bed with a hunting crop and Sergeant Henry threw himself on the bed. They also forced open the top drawer of the chest of drawers. Miss Knight confirmed that the noises produced were much the same as those she had heard originally.

Dr Spilsbury also confirmed that the bullet wounds were the only marks of violence on Baumberg and that there were no signs of a struggle on him.

When Muir concluded the case for the Crown, he repeated with great emphasis that the law assumed that homicide with a deadly weapon was murder unless it could be proved otherwise. Was there was any evidence from which it could be reasonably inferred that this particular act of homicide was either manslaughter or a justifiable act of self-defence? The answer was surely 'No'. There could be only one way out for my father – and it was that Baumberg had provoked him so much that he lost his control and shot him. If this was so, the verdict should be manslaughter. But there was not a shred of evidence to support this, and it was impossible to conceive that even a suggestion of such an attack took place. There was no other weapon in the room except the two the court had heard about – one in the possession of my father, and the other in its case in the open drawer, and apparently never taken out.

I have had as hard a task to perform as any advocate speaking for the Crown, in my belief, has ever had. A man would be less than human if he did not sympathise with all his manhood for a man like the prisoner trying to defend his wife against a scoundrel. But we in this court – and you members of the jury most of all – have a painful duty to perform. We must not allow our human feelings to prevent us doing our respective parts in the necessary administration of justice and the upholding of the law. We must not confuse a motive which

produces the desire for revenge with justification, or palliate murder to manslaughter. We live in times when it is more
than ever necessary to maintain the criminal law with firmness and justice. It is the
only protection of human life.

The law exists for the protection of
society from the more primitive passions of
mankind. Let the jury picture to themselves
the state of society after the war if a man
who was to be the sole arbiter and judge
of life and death was the man who came
home with a sense of wrong in his heart.
There would be no possible appeal against
such an injustice. That is why the law must
be upheld in this sad case. We must beware
lest by any act of ours we let loose these
primitive passions of revenge instead of
administering the law sturdily, setting our
hearts towards what is good for society, and
not allowing our sympathies to run riot for
what is good for the individual.

Muir's was a strong case, but he must have known
that, if this were a football match, he was playing
away with the crowd hardly cheering him on.

Simon now had to dismantle it. He did so by
going straight on the attack rather than defending
my father only with emotional excuses for his
conduct, though Baumberg was a villainous target
he could not resist for long. It was a brilliant effort

which made it easy for the all-male jury to absolve my father while still upholding those strict tenets of English law that Muir had emphasised so strongly. However much it looked as if my father's case was the first example of a *crime passionnel* in an English court, Simon denied it strongly. He refused to appeal to any 'unwritten law', and also cleverly refused to allow my father into the witness box where he might well have condemned himself under cross-examination. Those who packed the courtroom heard two giants of the courts in head-to-head combat, mediated by a judge of no less distinction. It was a great battle and, if it eventually resulted in complete victory for one side, there was plenty of blood spilled on both.

CHAPTER 7

THE SUMMING-UP

Making his final speech to the jury, Muir sounded at first as if he knew everything was against a conviction, except the real evidence in the case. He deferred quite abjectly to Simon, saying that the prisoner had the advantage of being defended by the most skilful advocate of the day. Few would quarrel with him, he added, if he put Sir John Simon's position even higher than that as a leading statesman of the day. The jury could take it for granted that my father would be defended with all due skill. But they'd better listen to him too, since he was basing his case solely on the evidence produced in court. He did not suppose for a moment that any attempt would be made by the defence to subvert the law. That was totally clear. Where one man killed another with a deadly weapon, it was murder. Unless it could be proved that provocation could reduce the charge to manslaughter or self-defence. In his submission, there was no evidence whatsoever even to hint at either proposition. The jury had to look at the facts and nothing else. If they did, my father was surely guilty of murder.

There was absolutely no evidence of any gross insult which might have made my father lose his control or of any mark on my father suggesting that he was attacked. There was evidence of a struggle of some severity in the room, it was true. But what was that struggle? Was it a struggle in which, the moment my father entered the room, he was endeavouring to force Baumberg on to the bed in order that he might inflict 'that disfiguring chastisement which he had said in his letter of 6 August that he meant to inflict'? He had provided himself with a formidable riding crop for that purpose.

Was it because my father found it too difficult to hold Baumberg down that he 'cut matters short and shot him'? If the Crown asked the jury to say that was what took place, their answer would surely be 'There is not a shred of evidence for it, and our verdict must be based on evidence.' Was it a struggle in which the prisoner was endeavouring to keep Baumberg from reaching his own revolver in the chest of drawers, in the course of which struggle Baumberg opened and shut the drawer in which the pistol was lying? Was it, in short, to prevent Baumberg taking that pistol that the prisoner shot him? That was easily the most favourable conjecture that the defence could put before the jury. And what would the jury's answer have to be to that? It would have to be the same answer as before – 'We cannot found our verdict on conjecture. We must have evidence.' There was no evidence whatsoever of that particular struggle, any more than there was of the other struggle he had mentioned.

Concluding, Muir said that he had as hard a task to perform as any advocate speaking for the Crown had ever had.

> A man would be less than human if he did not sympathise with all his manhood for a man like the prisoner attempting to defend his wife against a scoundrel. But we have in this court, and you members of the jury most of all, have a painful duty to perform. We must not allow our human feelings to prevent us doing our respective parts in the necessary administration of justice and the upholding of the law. We must not confuse a motive which produces the desire for revenge with justification or palliate murder to manslaughter.
>
> Gentlemen, we live in times when it is more than ever necessary to maintain the criminal law with firmness and justice. It is, after all, there for the protection of human life. There are at this very time hundreds of thousands of our best citizens going through an ordeal in foreign parts which must of necessity take away something from a man's regard for the sacredness of human life which a long series of peaceful years has made into one of the

strongest feelings of our nature. Hundreds of thousands of these men have left unprotected wives behind them. It is impossible to imagine that any one of them could have a greater wrong inflicted on him than has been inflicted on Lieutenant Malcolm. Many of them may have had as great a wrong done to them. But our law exists for the protection of society against the more primitive passions of mankind.

Picture to yourselves the state of our society in England after the war if a man who comes home with a sense of wrong in his heart is to be the sole and final judge of right or wrong. I say the final judge because, once his estimate of his wrong is carried into action by the punishment which he thinks is due for it, there is no appeal. The other man is dead. We must beware lest, by any act, we let loose those primitive passions of revenge instead of administering the law sturdily, setting our hearts towards what is good for society, and not allowing our sympathies to run riot for what is good for one individual.

I have had a hard task to perform. It is over, and now others must perform theirs. The Crown, I am sure, will not look in vain today to a British jury to uphold the standard of British criminal law which has always been upheld by good men and true.

It was an appeal to the jury's better instincts that was always likely to go unheeded, but it was one which laid out the facts of the case well enough. Firstly, that my father had in no way been harmed by Baumberg whose gun lay untouched in the drawer of his room. Thus self-defence was out of the question. If anyone was trying to defend himself, it was the surprised Baumberg, already the recipient of a severe beating from my father.

It was, however, curious that Muir had failed to wonder why my father had not gone into the witness box as the only one who could describe what had really happened. After Simon's speech, however, the judge did.

Simon began by saying that the jury had listened 'with strained attention' for close on two days to a recital of the evidence, and to two powerful speeches made on behalf of the Crown by Mr Muir. They all realised that when Muir said that his task was a hard one, he was not indulging in mere rhetoric but reminding the jury that he, like others concerned, had a duty to discharge. It was simply that justice must be done. Now, and at long last, the time had come when something could be said in defence of Douglas Malcolm.

On these same facts which have been proved before you, I ask you, as Douglas Malcolm's counsel, to say that a fair conclusion to be drawn in accordance with the law and in pursuance of your oaths is that he is guilty of no crime; that his actions from 15 July, when he first found his wife in Baumberg's room, to 14 August, when Baumberg lay dead, were actions without stain and without reproach. That they involve no condemnation according to the law which we are here to adminster, but that he acted under a compulsion which the law recognises and protects when at length, every other resource being exhausted, he was driven to defend his own life. But not just his own. He was also driven to defend the honour of his wife, which was dearer to him than his own.

My learned friend said something yesterday about the 'unwritten law'. I suppose he was referring to an expression sometimes used in another country to justify or explain the action of a jury which allows its sympathy or its passions to get the better of its reason and its duty. If that is what my learned friend means by the unwritten law, I make no appeal to it at all. I do not require to do so. It would, in fact, be contrary to my duty to do so and contrary to your duty to listen to me if I attempted it. This is a court of justice and you are sworn to do justice. And it is justice, and justice according to the law, which I stand here to ask you to mete out to the defendant.

My learned friend has made some observations to you in regard to the character of the law of murder. If we use words in their proper sense, the law of murder is, in substance, an unwritten law. That is to say the conception that is called murder, and is visited by the dreadful condemnation of death, is not defined in any statute, but has been built up and developed through the ages as part of the custom and common law of this country. Sir Edward Coke, one of the great judges of past times, declared that our common law was the perfection of reason. An important justification for relying on our common law in some of the most important branches of jurisprudence is precisely because it brings to each fresh case that arises – if and insofar as there is any need to do so – the application of old principles applied in the light of special facts.

I am bound to say that I do not know of any reported case which deals with the problem suggested by the facts in this case: namely, how you reconcile one of the highest and most important duties that a man can owe – the duty which is enshrined in our marriage service when he marries his wife – with taking the life of another man? A husband who unhappily finds that the wife he has been living with faithfully is being tempted by some would-be seducer has a method of discharging his duty which involves none of those awful questions of life and death. He discharges his duty by remaining with her, or taking her with him. And it is the poignant tragedy of this case that Lieutenant Malcolm, with the duty on him of protecting his wife, was deprived by the call of the only other duty he would recognise, that of defending his country abroad, of the chance to take her away with him to a place of safety. Nobody will ever hear me, who in times past have had some responsibility for the administration of the criminal law in this country, defend in a court of justice a review of the law of murder which will make light of the taking of human life. But, for my part, if such a situation were to arise and it became necessary to discuss and decide it, I should not be prepared to subscribe to the doctrine that, in a case where no other conceivable course can possibly save your wife – not indeed from unfaithfulness, but from destruction body and soul from the hands of a blackguard – that the duty of protecting the woman is thereupon dissolved, and that there is no other course within the common law of this country but that a husband should then retire and leave his wife to her fate. That is assuredly not the defence here.

Simon went on to say that he was confident he could show the jury a complete defence of Lieutenant Malcolm's actions, and that defence was that he took the life of Anton Baumberg because he was compelled to do so out of self-defence. 'What do we know of the two characters in this tragic drama?' he asked.

In June 1914, Lieutenant Malcolm was a partner in a well-known and prosperous business in the City. He was thirty years of age and a man of substance. In that month he married the woman that he adored, and there was then no duty lying on him but that of protecting and defending her, of loving and cherishing her as long as life should last. But within a few weeks of their wedding day war broke out in Europe, and this country was called upon to play its part, because it had to defend those who needed its protection, to be faithful to the vows which it had made, and to stand by its 'scraps of paper'.

The appeal which that terrible event made was bound to strike a response in the chivalrous heart of Douglas Malcolm. Within three days he was a member of his majesty's army. If he had sought excuse for hanging back, he might have found it. He was not a soldier by profession, he had important business interests to consider, he was a married man and his new wife needed him. We may fitly put on his lips the famous words said long ago by another soldier on going to the wars: 'I could not love thee, dear, so much, loved I not honour more.' Lieutenant Malcolm went immediately to do his duty in Egypt and in France. He left his bride at home that she might be safe.

And what do we know of the other man? He was a man about Malcolm's own age – a Russian by nationality, the worst of characters, passing under a false name and with a bogus title. He was associated with an infamous German woman who had since been dealt with in France as a spy. He might even have been involved in the treachery himself. He was without honest occupation, without ostensible means of living, one of those pieces of refuse carried along in the tide of great cities, living no one knew how.

Simon then spoke of 'this black, ugly, evil shadow which fell across the home in Cadogan Square where Malcolm had left his wife'. It did not appear that Mrs Malcolm had known Baumberg for more than two months. He remarked that Muir had said the defence could not rest on a sudden discovery by Malcolm of his wife's unfaithfulness. He then launched into a blatant appeal to the jury's sympathy, which must have been at least part of the reason he carried the day.

The prosecution reminded you of the declaration, chivalrous and ardent, as is everything which marks the attitude of Lieutenant Malcolm towards his wife, which the accused made when he was brought before the magistrate. Lieutenant Malcolm then spoke of a false and scurrilous slander. And I say here on his behalf that if the setting up of that slander, if the urging of that hypothesis, was the means by which he should be acquitted, then let him be condemned! He has never accepted it – never at any time has he accepted it, never at any moment has he contemplated that the purity of his wife has not been preserved unsmirched! And if there be, as some think, any technical view of the law which would make a sharp distinction in his favour by suggesting that he had the justification that his wife had fallen, I on his behalf say what I know he would insist on saying from the dock now were I not to say it for him – I deny, he denies, that there are any facts in this case which could justify that horrible conclusion, and he spurns with indignation the loophole, if loophole it be, which is indicated by that line of defence.

No, gentlemen, the defence here – and I am now going to develop it in order – the defence here is that, from the moment when he first had an altercation with this man Baumberg, right down to the moment when Baumberg lay dead in that room, the action which Lieutenant Malcolm took was forced upon him, and that so far from the history of his actions showing a murderous intent, he exhausted every means, he restrained himself in every way, and it was only when what Baumberg had threatened was found to be a reality, and the struggle in the little room became a case of Baumberg's life or his own, that he did what he was justified in doing and used his pistol.

The case I put to you is that Lieutenant Malcolm's course of action was a course which exhausted every alternative and which left him in the end under the immediate and instant peril of his life, compelled to take the life of his assailant. If you accept that, it will be your duty, as most assuredly it will be your privilege, to say that he is discharged from this criminal court as a man of honour, who has acted as all men of honour would wish to act – lawfully, courageously, bravely, devoted to the most sacred service which a husband can take upon him in an hour of peril.

Simon described how Baumberg had said that my father's challenge to a duel was 'not legal' and commented,

'The Devil was sick: The Devil a monk would be.' Lieutenant Malcolm took Baumberg's measure very exactly when he realised that if he was going to keep the man away, the one method of making certain that he would lie hidden was to send a challenge to him while he was still at Mrs Brett's Hampshire cottage. The man urged and prayed Mrs Brett to let him stay. He knew where he was safe. He knew that if only he could stay there he was not likely to come across Lieutenant Malcolm. Mrs Brett explained to you with tears in her eyes how she was forced to accept that position. She used an expression which I think must have struck you, that 'out of Christian charity' she let this man stay on.

Now in this order occurs this event. Baumberg, the person to whom this last document in addressed, buys a pistol. Not only does he buy it, but he is careful not to keep the fact to himself. After all, it is possible that if you are careful to let a woman's husband know that you have got a gun, the husband may think that the game is not worth the candle. Baumberg exhibits his pistol to the two ladies, Mrs Brett and Mrs Malcolm. He says to Mrs Brett, 'I have bought this in case Lieutenant Malcolm attacks me. It is loaded.' But he says more than that. He says to these two women, 'If Malcolm lays a finger on me I will use it.'

Simon described Malcolm's frenzied search of London, his discovery of de Borch's whereabouts and his arrival 'at that room of death' as 'Inspector Quinn'.

Shooting? Murder? Not at all. I submit to you that it is as plain as any inference reasonably drawn from plain facts in a court of justice ever can be, that Lieutenant Malcolm entered the room with that whip for the purpose of giving the man who had soiled his wife's reputation the flogging which he justly deserved and which he had said he would give him. What else would he take the whip for? People bent on using revolvers do not want whips. Baumberg had not got a whip. What is the good of a whip if you are determined to use a revolver?

I submit a second inference to you. I address it not to your sympathy, nor to your passions but to your judgement. I submit that it can be inferred with reasonable certainty that the drawer which, as you now know, contained this pistol which Baumberg had bought for the purpose of using against Malcolm if he attempted to touch him, was opened after, and not before, Malcolm entered the room. I will tell you why I say so.

No one can surely doubt that the drawer was opened for the purpose of getting at the revolver, for there was nothing in it that was of any use to a man who was either going to bed or getting up from bed, except the revolver. A man who is dressed in nothing but the upper half of a suit of pyjamas does not want a tie-pin or a tie, and the only articles of wearing apparel in that drawer were a tie-pin and a tie.

You remember I asked the policeman who searched the room where Baumberg's clothes were, and it appeared that his clothes were not in that drawer at all. Some of them were in a cupboard and some of them were elsewhere. Now, if it is clear that the drawer was opened because the revolver was in it, it is, I submit to you, practically certain that it was opened after Baumberg discovered that the man who was entering his room was Malcolm.

If you want to pass the night with the protection of a revolver at your side, you might keep it under your pillow or you might put it on a chair close by your pillow. You may remember that I called attention to the fact that there was a chair immediately at the side of the bed close to the pillow. The revolver was not lying there, and for the best of all reasons – if Lieutenant Malcolm is away in France it is no doubt a very good thing to be provided with a revolver in case of ultimate need, but when you are not likely to need it until he comes back, I submit to you that the inference is an inference which any sensible man would draw, apart altogether from his sympathies in his case, namely that the drawer was opened after Baumberg discovered to his horror that the man who had come into his room was none other than the husband of Mrs Malcolm.

If that drawer was opened by Baumberg after Malcolm had entered the room because he wanted to get at the revolver within it, how is it that he did not get at the revolver? It is the action of an instant. You will remember that I asked one of the police officers whether the revolver did not so lie inside the open drawer that it was immediately to be got by dropping your hand upon it, and he told us that this was so. In another instant it would have been in the man's hand. It matters very little to me at what precise moment in the course of the struggle he approached most nearly to the revolver. There is evidence that would justify you in supposing that he attempted to get at it at once, and was then foiled and perhaps driven back towards the bed. At any rate that was not the end of this struggle on the floor of the room.

Miss Knight is perfectly clear that there was a commotion that went on for an appreciable time. How is that consistent with the theory that Lieutenant Malcolm enters the room with his pistol all ready to fire, and the moment he has got a clear view of his enemy, wreaks his vengeance upon him? It is wholly inconsistent with it. In the course of the struggle, Baumberg would get to the place where the drawer was, and is it not also perfectly certain that if he had been allowed one moment in which he could, in fact, possess himself of his weapon, he would have used it, as he had vowed he would use it if a finger was laid upon him by Lieutenant Malcolm? And, as was pointed out, I think in answer to a question from my lord, it might have been used even without taking off the leather cover which contained it.

The sounds which Miss Knight heard, like the whip striking the bedrail, showed the struggle had raged until Baumberg was perhaps only five feet from the open drawer where the revolver lay. Two steps more and his hand would have been on the weapon.

It being abundantly clear that a struggle was going on – it being proved before you that Baumberg was man who had bought and exhibited a formidable weapon by which he had vowed he would defend himself – it being proved that the drawer was open and the weapon lying in it, although the moment happily never arose when Baumberg was actually able to succeed in getting it into his hand – is not the conclusion that follows irresistible and overwhelming?

First, that Lieutenant Malcolm did not enter that room for the purposes of murder, but for the purpose of chastisement. The conclusion, secondly, that the man upon whom he was going to visit that righteous thrashing was a man who made desperate efforts to get at the only thing in the room which would save his skin. Thirdly, that he was within an ace of success. And fourthly, that unless at that moment Lieutenant Malcolm was to hold up his hands and retreat as a result of this ruffian's threat, he was driven in the heat and impulse of that struggle – not as part of the purpose for which he entered the room, but as a necessary consequence of what occurred in the room – then and there in a moment of time to use this revolver with which he had so prudently provided himself, knowing as he must have known, and as he said in the letter to his wife, that the other man was likely to be armed.

I am not going to harrow your feelings by reading the letter – it has already been read twice – which he wrote to his dear wife. It will long remain in the annals of this court, annals which so often contain chapters of pathos and of tragedy, a noble monument to what a chivalrous man may say to his wife when he may be facing death to defend her. It contains one passage which is important as bearing on your conclusion in this case. It contains the statement that he is going to give Baumberg a thrashing, it contains the statement that he has probably got a gun, it contains the statement that if he has, Lieutenant Malcolm might be the first to fall.

Now, gentlemen, if there be any document in this case which you may confidently treat as a record of true emotion, as a real revelation of Lieutenant Malcolm's mind, it is that document. Not only because it was addressed to his wife, not only because declarations made by people with sudden death staring them in the face have a special sanctity, but for a much more obvious reason than that – because Lieutenant

Malcolm kept it in his pocket, and had it not been for the intervention of the police, nobody would ever have known what he had written unless he had been killed.

That is the view of the facts which I present to you. And that view amounts to a verdict of innocence, and that is the verdict I ask you to pronounce. It is a reasonable view, and apart from the duty that lies on you to put a construction on incidents of doubtful import which is favourable to the accused, you, I am sure, must rejoice that a way is open to you that is indicated, justified and authorised by the law itself. It leads to the only conclusion that responds to the promptings of your hearts.

You have the undoubted opportunity to reach a verdict strictly on the facts. The way is open to you, and I ask you to take it. Let that man among you who is prepared openly to avow that in like circumstances he would not wish to show the courage and chivalry of Douglas Malcolm cast the first stone. No, gentlemen, rather let us, who are actors in the last scene of this tragedy, help to restore this unhappy wife to her faithful husband by showing her that he is a champion of whom she may well be proud.

I am not asking you to disregard your oaths, or to set at naught the law under which we live. But the law is the servant and not the master of our community. It exists to foster and preserve what is brave and noble, to be a terror to evil-doers, and a shield to such as do well. And it is the particular glory of our English law that in these dread matters of life and death it leaves the final decision, not to the pedantic application of some written code, not even to the learning and impartiality of our judges, but to the sense of justice and to the sense of duty of twelve citizens chosen by lot to represent the community as whole, relying upon them that they will preserve and that they will apply that law which is the foundation of all our liberties.

Gentlemen, Lieutenant Malcolm is here before you in the clothes of a civilian. It is for you to say – for the great and final responsibility is yours – whether he shall pass from this place to the condemned cell to put on the shameful garments of the gaol, or whether, in the words of the juryman's oath, you have sworn to make 'true deliverance between our sovereign Lord the King and the prisoner at the Bar', will return him to the service of His Majesty and bid him put on again the uniform which he has done nothing to disgrace and so much to justify.

Douglas Malcolm awaits your verdict

with a quiet mind conscious that whatever that verdict may be he has protected the honour of his nearest and dearest, confident that whatever record meets the light, he shall never be shamed.

The moment Simon stopped speaking, there was loud and prolonged applause from the courtroom which Judge McCardie tried to quell without success. A witness present timed it at over three minutes before silence was restored. McCardie then started his own summing-up, trying immediately to dampen down the emotion that Simon's quietly spoken appeal had caused.

He said that the defendant was charged with the gravest of crimes. If a man intentionally destroyed the life of another without lawful excuse, he was guilty of that crime. If a man took a pistol without lawful excuse, and fired at another intending to kill, or to inflict grievous bodily harm on him, and the victim died, that was clearly murder. Was Lieutenant Malcolm guilty of that offence? The case must on no account be decided on bias, on natural sympathy or on the mere appeal and eloquence of a distinguished counsel. It must be determined on facts and in strict accordance with the law of the land. In some special cases where a man did that which prima facie was murder, the law enabled a jury to say it was manslaughter only. This was where the provocation was so grave and so sudden as to leave a jury to think that his self-control was overthrown and his capacity for judgement destroyed.

If a husband suddenly discovered his wife in the act of adultery and he killed her or the man involved, the jury might find that the provocation was such as to justify them in finding a verdict of manslaughter only. But if a man is told by others that his wife has committed adultery, and he then decides to seek out and kill the adulterer and deliberately to destroy him, then by the law of the country he would undoubtedly be guilty of murder. If the law were otherwise, grave consequences would ensue. We should not be subject to the law as it is administered in the King's courts. Instead, we should be subject to the law of the individual, which is sometimes called the unwritten law but in others can only be called lynch law.' I desire to say,' said the judge, 'in the most clear and unmistakable terms, that this so-called unwritten law does not exist in England. It is opposed to the most elementary principles of British justice – namely open trial and unbiased adjudication.'

Then came the most significant part of his view of the case, one which was by no means an obvious thing for a judge to say at that time:

A husband has no property in the body of his wife. It is her own body and nobody else's. He cannot imprison her and he cannot chastise her. If she chooses not to live with him, he cannot and nor can the courts compel her to do so. She is the mistress of her own physical destiny. If she sins and the husband can prove it, he may obtain a divorce. But if she decides to give her body to another, then the husband is not entitled to murder the lover, either to punish the sin or to secure its correction.

The law of England is settled, and you and I are here to administer it as it stands, and with loyalty to the oaths we have taken. You, the jury, would do well to remember that the supremacy of the law is of far more importance than any temporary indulgence of natural temper.

He then suggested that if a proper verdict was forthcoming, and a proper verdict could certainly be my father's guilt, the jury could be assured that it might not necessarily mean either a hanging or even a long term of imprisonment.

I do not forget, and nor should you, that beyond this court, which must administer the law in accordance with the facts, there stands the right of the Crown to show mercy. If you consider it your duty to find a verdict of murder or manslaughter against the defendant, the Crown through its advisers can still consider whether any mitigation can be extended to Lieutenant

Malcolm. The duty of administering the law rests on us – the exercise of mercy is the prerogative of the Crown.

It is said, and indeed has been proved, that the dead man was not an Englishman. True, but it matters not in what realm a man has been born. It matters not what foreign sun has burnt on his cheek. The moment he sets foot on British soil, he falls within the King's peace and the shackles of foreign nationality do not prevent him from demanding to be protected by the ordinary rules of British justice. It has further been said that this dead man was a criminal. If he was, let him be judged and punished according to law. The fact that he might have been a blackmailer, a white slave trafficker or a spy would never justify a murder by the hands of an irresponsible man.

If you think that the defendant honestly believed that the dead man meant to shoot him and he fired to save himself from grave personal injury, or even to save his life, I think you are entitled to find a verdict of not guilty. But you must remember that it was not the dead man who visited Malcolm but Malcolm who visited the dead man. He went there with a whip. But he also went there with a pistol. And he announced, 'I will thrash him until I have maimed him for life.' The question might well have been raised by the Counsel for the Crown whether Baumberg was not himself entitled, if Malcolm went there with a whip to maim him for life, to fire his own gun in order to protect himself. That point has not been raised, though many might feel that it should have been.

Therefore I say you are entitled to find a verdict of acquittal if you are satisfied that Malcolm honestly believed that Baumberg was about to seize a pistol and shoot at him – that is, if you believe that he honestly shot him to protect his own life.

When you recall that in the early hours of 14 August the defendant, who is setting up a plea of self-defence, mounted the steps of that house with a whip in one hand and a revolver in the other, it is in his favour, strongly in his favour, that he had not previously threatened the life of his rival. He had threatened to thrash him, but he had not threatened his life. He had written two challenges to a duel, but the letter contained no threat of murder or killing.

It is quite clear that the dead man had a pistol and would have used it if he could have laid his hands upon it. That pistol was loaded and lay in an open drawer not far from the bed on which the Russian lay. But there is only one man living who could now tell us what actually happened in that room, and that man has not gone into the witness box. Why not? He is physically able to do so. There was nothing to prevent him unless it was the fear that his testimony might in some way condemn him. He stood indicted with the gravest charge and yet offered not one word of testimony. He has asked the jury to guess and to conjecture things which, if he had desired, he could have proved on oath.

The result of this grave omission was that there was no evidence whatsoever that the dead man even tried to get at his own pistol in the open drawer. There was no evidence whatsoever that he threatened to use it. There was no real evidence even that the pistol was in the room. The whole thing has been left to conjecture. Added to that, there was not a single mark on the face or body of Lieutenant Malcolm which might have suggested a struggle.

The jury, McCardie said, had to deal with facts, not inferences. And the evidence showed them that 'the Russian' was not a muscular man, whereas the defendant was a fit and trained soldier in full possession of his physical power. He had overpowered the other man once and could there be any doubt that he could also do that again?

The defendant went to his room with a whip

and a gun at a time when he must have known that the Russian would be in bed. He had been told the night before that Baumberg came in at all hours. Lieutenant Malcolm was fully clothed and armed, whereas Baumberg had only got on a pyjama jacket.

> Now what you have got to ascertain is this – did the Russian, when the defendant had overcome him, attempt to fire his own gun, or did the defendant prevent him even trying to get the pistol in the drawer? This is what you have to determine. I cannot and would not instruct you how to do so, or on what verdict you should decide upon. I can merely advise, and even then you do not have to take that advice. But I now rely on you to come to a just and equitable verdict.

The jury retired to consider their verdict at 4.45 p.m. on the second day of the trial. And to the surprise of everyone in court who had stood up or gone out to await the verdict, they were absent for only twenty minutes. 'The early return of the jury', wrote the *Telegraph*,

> took everyone by surprise. The judge resumed his seat on the bench, and the prisoner took up a position in the front of the dock. The eyes of all in court were upon

the jurors as their names were called in order to see that all were present.

When the clerk of the court asked them whether they found Douglas Malcolm guilty or not guilty of murder, and the foreman replied 'not guilty', there was a loud out-burst of applause from those who had hastily reassembled in court. This time it lasted even longer than the applause with which Simon's speech was greeted, and the ushers tried in vain to quell it.

Cheers within the court were long sustained, in spite of the appeals of the judge and ushers for silence, and they quickly found an echo outside the building. It was when the verdict was given that the pent-up feelings of the public outside found expression. There were loud cheers, and the voices of women mingled with those of men. On the bench sat the judge, solemn and regretful at what was occurring in his courtroom. In the dock stood the prisoner, looking towards the bench with a serious expression, yet one which indicated feelings of relief. The ushers exclaimed 'Silence', but for some time they were unheeded. Eventually silence was restored. Then the judge expressed his sorrow at the disturbance, adding that proceedings in a court of justice should be conducted quietly and with dignity.

The prisoner was then discharged and, as he retired below, there was another outburst of cheering, which was finally taken up by the crowd of thousands outside the court, where the result of the trial had instantly become known.

The Times added even more dramatic detail:

On the instant [of the verdict] a woman's voice from the back of the court called loudly, 'Oh, thank God!' Then someone in the gallery started, not a confused roar of applause, but a lead for three cheers which were immediately given. By this time nearly everyone in court was on his or her feet, and the cheering was deafening. So loud was it that none of the cries for order could be heard.

When quiet had finally been restored, Mr Justice McCardie said, 'I am sorry the traditions of this court have been stained by this applause. It is essential that the proceedings in a court of justice should be conducted in a quiet and dignified manner.'

The clerk asked the foreman [of the jury], who was still standing, 'Do you find the prisoner guilty of any other crime?' and the foreman answered emphatically, 'No.'

The applause from the courtroom was

then taken up in the corridors and spread to the street outside, where a huge crowd had collected. Lieutenant Malcolm, perceptibly paler than he was earlier in the afternoon, stood up and waited quietly for a few minutes before he followed the warder down the dock stairs . . .

The *Daily Mirror* added, 'For quite five minutes pandemonium reigned. Solemn-looking ushers raised their arms and appealed for order in vain. The noise was deafening. The scene resembled the unrestrained jubilation of a pre-war football match – a man seated at the extreme end of the judge's bench cheered and waved a straw hat in a most frantic way.'

As my father stood to leave the court, Muir rushed over to him and smilingly shook his hand. It was perfectly clear where his sympathies lay, even if he thought my father guilty. When my father left the building, accompanied by Sir John Simon, he was mobbed by a crowd of several thousand, among whom were many women and a number of serving soldiers.

He shouted to Simon at one point as they were both trying to get through the crowd, 'Can I say something now? I want to tell them the truth.' 'No,' said Simon, emphatically. 'You must remain as silent as you were in court.'

'Very well,' my father said. 'You saved my life. I'll not go against what you say.' It was probably the wisest decision he had made in his life.

He made no statement whatever to the waiting press – owing to the fact, reported the *Mirror* apparently without its tongue in its cheek, that as a serving soldier he was now responsible to his superior military officers. That must have been Simon's idea. The paper added, however, that it had been informed that the lieutenant was extremely gratified by the way in which Sir John Simon 'absolutely cleared his wife's good name'.

Finally parting from Simon, he drove away in a taxi by himself. As he did so, the paper reported, a woman shouted after him, 'Bravo, Malcolm, bravo!'

CHAPTER 8

AFTER THE TRIAL

There was no national paper that did not contain lengthy comments about the trial and its result. All of them seemed to approve of the verdict as much as the public. Comments varied from the hyperbolic to the studiedly pontifical, praising both Simon and Judge McCardie. Given the melodramatic nature of the case, the popular enthusiasm for its outcome might also have happened today. But few leader writers now would have found it necessary to expound on the verdict in the way they did then.

The *Daily Mirror* described the trial as 'probably the most sensational love tragedy ever unfolded in a criminal court in this country' and commented that 'the story of how Lieutenant Malcolm shot the bogus Count in order to save his wife's honour appealed especially to women'.

The Times, in a leader after the trial, betrayed some of the innate prejudices of the time that had enabled my father to leave the court a free man to such acclaim. It made effective mincemeat of the probable truth with a highly coloured diatribe that romanticised the case even more

184

than Simon had quietly but brilliantly managed in the more emotional part of his closing address. It was almost as if the leader writer were reviewing a particularly romantic novel or play. In fact, the whole affair must have seemed at the time rather better than most fiction, and possibly stranger.

While the war upon which our fortunes are staked passes through a phase bewildering and momentous, the attention of the public has been engaged by the trial of a young officer on a charge of murder. However intense, however busy our patriotism, few of us can resist and none of us need apologise for an eager interest in the case of Lieutenant Malcolm.

A man suffering a shameful wrong, a man driven by the vice and weakness of others to action imperilling his life and his good name, must needs command our sympathy, and it happens that every circumstance in this man's fate combines to display a character singularly appealing. In the story are crowded all the elements with which artists are wont to excite the imagination – true love and degrading passion, hideous villainy, miserable weakness, the strength that shrinks from no danger and admits no defeat. Melodramatic violence is mingled with dramatic contrast and conflict of character, until both alike yield to the throb of tragedy.

But there is, besides and beyond all this, another factor which makes the trial memorable. Though the case offered an advocate every temptation to appeal to reckless sentiment and lawless emotion, though the circumstances gave occasion for moral indignation which might have swayed even a judicial mind, neither the defence nor the prosecution chose to rely upon anything not found within the written law and the sworn evidence. Neither sympathy with a man much wronged nor untimely censure of the infamy of the dead tinged the calm impartiality of the judge's directions to the jury . . . The records of the Malcolm trial will form an historic example of the temper and methods of our courts. Here is no case of vengeance or violence for the sake of gratifying rage. The sternest moralist must confess that the story of Lieutenant Malcolm shows us a man of fine honour and lofty spirit, to whom passion meant faith and devotion, and grant no grudging admiration to a man who, tortured by a cruel wrong, only thought of saving the woman he had trusted from the ghastly fate to which, like a dumb creature fascinated by a beast of prey, she was faltering, paralysed in mind and will.

The leader went on to describe Baumberg as 'one of those creatures whom the French novelists of thirty years ago were fond of painting, the offspring of vice born to revenge himself by spreading his own corruption upon the world which had created him. A man of some prensence but no strength, he was without any trace of intellectual distinction. He was not merely a libertine but steeped in crime which vice itself holds infamous, a purveyor for the 'white slave' traffic, the helpmeet of spies.' It ended, 'In our natural satisfaction at the verdict we shall do well to remember how it was reached. The jury, whose duty it was to resolve the question, has declared that the evidence which pointed to a struggle and an act of self-defence was conclusive. The case is judged. The outburst of cheering when the trial was over, a natural but undesirable ebulition of emotion, should not obscure the fact that it was judged according to law.'

But was it? Simon stretched the law a bit, appealing as much to the jury's emotions while appearing to deal solely with the facts of the case. The sometimes almost reluctant prosecution by Muir, the anti-Baumberg tone of the police evidence and the obvious feelings of a patriotic wartime jury that took so little time to find a verdict, make the idea that the law was strictly interpreted at least questionable.

If it was indeed the first case of *crime passionnel* in a British court, as many felt at the time, it was not to be the last. Similar cases were later heard both before and after the war was concluded. It was, however, easily the most notorious. Private soldiers who came home to find their loved ones with another were treated with less respect. According to the records, they were seldom given the ultimate penalty for murder. They were, however, either imprisoned for manslaughter or bound over to keep the peace for a number of years.

In the immediate aftermath of the trial only the *Manchester Guardian*, which was to become the paper for which I worked for so many years, cast some doubt upon the verdict. But even then, the paper did not evince much sympathy either for the dead man or for the woman who apparently loved him. The leader started shrewdly enough, and with some wit, but then appeared almost as conventional in its responses as that of *The Times*, though it did place in its European context the idea of the *crime passionnel*.

> None of the characters in this dramatic story belongs to a conventional type. The figure of the husband is dignified by the purity and sincerity of his passion for his wife and by his touching faith in her honour, but he is Gallic rather than English in his conduct, and he has none of the phlegm that is supposed to be part of our character. The man who was killed was an

adventurer of a particularly unclean type, and one of the puzzles of the case is to understand how a woman capable of inspiring such devotion in her husband should ever have fancied that she preferred a scoundrel like de Borch.

In France, these '*drames passionnels*' are often in the courts. Half a generation ago, the English papers were constantly jesting at what they then regarded as the extreme sentimentality of Paris juries and it is only the other month that the '*Temps*' printed a column of elaborate satire on a verdict of not guilty on a charge of murder against a woman who had shot her husband. In France it is nearly always the woman who gets the sympathy of the jury. In the Malcolm case, it was the man. And it is to be doubted whether any verdict has ever given rise to such demonstrations of joy as were witnessed when the verdict in this case was announced. Mr Justice McCardie, whose conduct of this case was finely dignified, stigmatised the applause as a stain on the record of the court, and his rebuke was not merely formal. It is evident from his summing-up that he was worried at being in an atmosphere as unusual as this in the administration of British law.

Mr Muir, the prosecutor for the Crown,

put his point a little crudely but quite sincerely when he said that this was a time when it was above all necessary to insist on respect for the sanctity of human life, and the judge fully agreed with him on this point. While it is unfair to question the verdict of a jury, a verdict of guilty followed by a pardon would not have caused surprise, and it would have led to rather less moralising on the curious atmosphere of this case than the verdict actually given. Apart from the more rhetorical passages which we do not greatly admire, Sir John Simon's speech for the defence was an exceedingly fine effort. While expressly excluding from the case any appeal to the 'unwritten law' which, as the judge pointed out, is quite unrecognised by English courts of justice, he still managed to enlist on behalf of the accused man all the sympathies which abroad have been held to justify the 'unwritten law'. He had a case which was extraordinarily strong on the sentimental side and very weak on the side of the facts. He was careful not to introduce any new principle of law or to try to extend the doctrine of justifiable homicide in any way.

The burden of the defence was that Lieutenant Malcolm killed Baumberg under circumstances that would have justified anyone killing him – namely not in order to save his honour or to protect the honour of his wife, but in order to save his own life. This defence placed a tremendous burden on the facts, the more so since Lieutenant Malcolm, who alone knew them, was not called to give evidence. But, as it turned out, the facts managed to carry the burden and Sir John's bold course was justified. He had also the consolation that he had strained no aspect of English law and introduced no new one. But apart from its human aspects, the case will go down as one of the most important in the annals of English justice. So far as Lieutenant Malcolm is concerned the result is substantially right. And yet, when all is said and done, many people, like ourselves, would prefer that the result had been reached in another way.

The law has not been strained. The facts were, if not strained, at least overburdened. But if something had to be strained to secure moral, as opposed to legal justice – the two are not always the same – we would have preferred the strain being put on the royal prerogative of pardon.

The whole trial took place, however, in the earliest days of what we would now call feminism, when a number of women who had distinguished themselves in life were beginning to question a great deal – for instance, the fact that there were no women on the jury in the case because they were not allowed such a privilege at that time. And several articles, written by women after the trial, sensed that something might be wrong with the general public's attitude to the case, and towards the woman involved in it. One unidentified writer, making tacit reference to the case, began,

What, and whose, is a woman's honour? Any actor in melodrama knows he has only to mention the thing to be sure of a good round of applause from the gallery. Just now there seems to be a dangerous tendency for the melodramatic habit to invade real life and for the conventional recklessness of the gallery to prevail. It is an odd symptom of disordered times. The strain of war has burst much that was glamorous and rent many illusions. Women have developed enormously on their human, as opposed to merely feminine side . . . But alongside this development there seems to be running another – a sort of specialisation in femininity. The frothy flood of ephemeral clothes is among the minor symptoms of this specialisation.

A much more serious one is the spreading of a lapse into the medieval idea that a woman's personal chastity is the affair, or the asset, of her male relatives, and that its protection is a matter beyond civil law . . . Has a woman no honour save that which is involved in sexual relations? . . . Why should we lose sight of the fact that, in matters of human relations also, she is responsible? She is, as Mr Justice McCardie declared to a jury recently, 'mistress of her own destiny'. Should there not be an outcry against the impression that she is not?

Women have for centuries struggled for the human privilege of standing morally and legally on their own two feet. They are still struggling. Under English law, a wife is not the property of her husband. He may not shut her up, he may not beat her, he may not even compel her to live in his house if she prefers to live elsewhere. Is she then going to allow it to be taken for granted that her 'honour' may rest not on her own intelligence and honesty, but on the strength of his arm?

This article, signed by E. S. H., received a forthright response the next day in another piece from a reporter which included quotes from several activist women, all of whom objected to the triumphalist tone of the press concerning the verdict.

Miss Nina Boyle, the novelist, lecturer, suffragette and at that time secretary of the Women's

Freedom League, reported to be just back from nursing in Serbia, agreed:

> I regard the Malcolm case as an insult to every woman in England and a disgrace to the country, the courts, the Bench and the Bar. In my opinion the most serious failure in the whole case is that the defence was conducted by a man who is an ex-Home Secretary and may some day hold office again. What he said in defence of Lieutenant Malcolm – that he shot Baumberg in self-defence and also in defence of his wife's honour – was totally insufferable.

The popular novelist Gertie Wentworth-James concurred:

> Every woman is completely the mistress of her own destiny, which may, in this sense, be called inclination so far as matters of love and passion are concerned. No woman, unless forced, yields anything to a man unless she wants to. This being the case, the very idea of a woman needing any assistance in the defence of her honour seems as grotesque as the exploits of a hero in a melodrama who, single-handed, wipes out a large detachment of a fully armed enemy.

Sylvia Pankhurst, a member of the famous suffragette family, the daughter of Emmeline and sister of Christabel, was a little less sweeping. 'All these cases depend upon various circumstances. There may be instances where the man is to blame and others where the woman is at fault. If a woman is the victim of superior force, then she is entitled to the fullest protection that the law, not her husband's riding whip and gun, can give.' And Fryn Tennyson Jesse, the novelist and playwright, who was the great-niece of the poet Tennyson and one of the few women war correspondents, commented,

I deprecate the separation of human beings into two classes, and labelled men and women when the question of honour is involved. Honour surely is, like all the qualities worth having, not only irrespective of sex, but a thing to which each human being is responsible themselves and to the community but to no one other person. To take one quality, giving it peculiar significance, and then invest some other than the exerciser of it with propriety rights, is absurd. By a woman's honour is meant, if the expression be analysed, the right, until marriage, of society to a certain standard from a woman. After marriage, the right of some man to claim that standard. There are only two rights – that which one owes to oneself and that which one owes to the community. The less one thinks of those which other people owe to oneself, the better.

But the argument did not go away. Gertie Wentworth-James returned to the attack on the following day:

Mr Justice McCardie has just said that woman is 'mistress of her own destiny'. So she is, and the recent attempt by Sir John Simon to suggest otherwise should be refuted without delay. Such early Victorian shams and pretences should be done away with. Men themselves must be protected from them, for it is a certain and definite fact that no woman ever enters into a love affair or intrigue with any man unless she intends to do so . . . of course a woman may become entangled with a man she comes to detest. But even when this pitiful thing occurs, the woman is the consenting party, and it is not that she is so weak and frail as to require the protection of a strong manly arm and a firm manly brain!

If inquiry were made into most cases where a woman has presumably fallen into the power of a man, there is very little doubt that discoveries would be made concerning letters she has answered, telephone calls which she has put in, appointments she has kept and outings which she has shared, because no man ever continues to pursue unless he is encouraged, or permitted, to do so. Quite likely in the past she has actually believed that she needed a strong protecting arm to keep her doing what she shouldn't do.

Today she knows she doesn't ... a woman needs love and tenderness and care (oh, how passionately and yearningly she needs them!) but she doesn't need anyone to prevent her losing hold of her own honour. This, thank God, she can now do for herself. Lieutenant Malcolm is apparently a hero to the public for saving his wife's honour in the simplest possible way – by shooting the man she stated that she loved. I fear we have a long way to go before such actions are properly condemned for what they are – insupportable in the modern age.

This 'modern age' of 1917 now seems long ago. I would not wish to belittle my father for his constant talk of 'honour', or to mock my mother's involvement in an affair with a man like Baumberg. But it is difficult not to wonder what possessed my father, even in his natural anxiety and emotional panic, to behave as he did. It is also not easy to contemplate exactly what my mother saw in Baumberg, even if he was not the devil incarnate depicted in court and in the press. That both of them had been foolish is obvious. There, however, but for the grace of God, go a good many of us.

About a year after I found Lustgarten's book hidden among my father's clothes, the phone rang when both my parents were out. 'Is this the home of Captain Malcolm?' When I replied that it was, but that he was out, the voice said, 'Would you be his son? My name is Simon – Lord Simon – and I defended your father in a case of mine. Has he told you about it?' I told Simon, untruthfully, that he had. 'Then I need to ask you another question. This was one of my best-known cases, and I'd like to include it in my memoirs. Do you think your father or mother would mind?' My answer was that they would, even if, as he then suggested, the names in the case were changed. 'Very well,' said Simon, 'I'll not write about it. Please be assured that I won't bother you or your parents again.'

But he thought better of that decision. In a letter dated 26 May, 1951, he wrote to my mother:

Dear Mrs Malcolm,
    You may remember me as the K.C. who successfully defended your husband at the Old Bailey in 1917.
    I am writing my memoirs, mostly polit-

ical, but the publishers want me to include a specimen of my advocacy when at the Bar. The most suitable example would be that speech, but I would alter the names, saying for example 'Captain Unwin' for 'Lieutenant Malcolm' and so on, as it is all now happily forgotten and I would not for a moment wish to distress you or others who remain.

Will you kindly let me know if you see any objection to this course?

My mother must quickly have replied to him because on 1 June, he sent her another letter.

Dear Mrs Malcolm,

I am so glad I wrote to you, because your reply makes me feel sure that I ought not to revive the memory of long ago, when I tried to serve both you and your husband, and I shall not include the case in my book. So feel quite at ease about this. It has always been a happiness to me that this domestic storm blew over, and I would not on any account do anything to distress you – or to complicate the start of your son at Oxford, which I love so well. I hope he is happy, with Merton going Head of the River!

Not long afterwards, my father called me into his bedroom at around 9 p.m. He was sitting up in bed pretending to read a book. He looked nervous and distressed, but came straight to the point. 'I've got to tell you something . . . and you may not like what you're going to hear. This is very difficult for me because I know you will think very badly of me. But I must tell you – and I should have done so before – I once killed a man who was having an affair with your mother. It was a stupid thing to do. But I meant to give him a good thrashing and it ended up differently. I said it was self-defence at the time and I got off. 'But I shot him, and that was that. I was very much in love with your mother then. But please don't tell her I told you. Never mention it to her. She doesn't want you to know.'

All I could muster in reply was, 'Yes, I knew already. Lord Simon rang up to ask whether you would mind if he included the case in his memoirs, and I told him that you would. But don't worry. I don't think badly of you. If I'd had a gun, I'd have probably done the same.'

'Really?' my father said. 'Do you think so? I've been awfully worried about telling you. But, my God, I was foolish. It ruined both our lives, you know. Ruined, damn it, ruined.'

It was as much of a relief to me as it was to him that he'd finally told me. He never spoke of it again. Nor did I ever tell my mother that I knew of the case. It explained much but not everything about their unhappiness. I reflected that even without such a trauma they would have found themselves unhappy together soon enough. But it clearly went so deeply into their lives that, however curious I was, I knew that my silence was more or less imperative.

I was neither traumatised nor shocked by the revelations. The story seemed to me to come from another era, which I hardly recognised and of which I had no experience whatsoever. Besides, the two young marrieds who went through the trauma of the killing seemed to have no real connection to the sad, elderly people they had now become. But they were my parents and I was fond of them both, so I was saddened when I finally discovered the answer to the puzzle of their subsequent life together. It seemed to have, however, very little relevance to me. I found out some time later that, in fact, it did.

CHAPTER 9

BACK TO THE FRONT

My father went back to France almost immediately after the trial. My mother went back to her mother's. A few weeks later, after the Armistice was signed, he wrote an extraordinary letter to his own much-loved and by now elderly and infirm mother. Amazingly enough her family had seen to it that she was kept in the dark about the trial both before it started and while it was going on. The whole household had conspired to keep the daily papers away from her, finally sending her off with a friend to a remote cottage in the Highlands of Scotland for a 'holiday'. She thus knew nothing of the case until it had been completed, and then only in the briefest detail. She had said to my father 'How horrible for you!' I was told by a cousin of mine who remembered the occasion, 'but of course you were completely innocent.' The letter my father wrote to her began,

My dearest mother,
    I hope you are keeping well, and free from influenza. I got it the day after the Armistice

202

was signed, but it was not very bad except for a high temperature. We were fortunately near a village, so I got a bed in a cottage and stayed there for three days and am just about all right now, though still rather weak. However, I'm feeling better every day.

We are in Hautmont just a few miles south of Maubeuge and Mons. We were in action till the last minute almost and were all too thankful for words when we were told hostilities had ceased. The strain of the last three months has been very severe – by the by, I am a Captain now. I have been Acting Captain for the last six weeks, but have only just been gazetted. I was commanding this battery for a short time, as the Major was wounded near Vesle and Au Tetre Farm, the latter a well-known place in 1914.

We were stuck for ten days in a horrible position between that village and the farm whilst the infantry were preparing to attack Solesmes and get over the railway. We were simply shelled day and night. The only shelter we had was holes dug under hedges – it wasn't so bad during the day, but it was beastly at night, wandering about the country dodging shells till he stopped for an hour or two before starting again at dawn.

We lost a good many men – I've hardly got anything fit to wear as I had just crept out of my valise to take the usual dawn harassing fire (we used to fire every morning at dawn to make the Germans think we were going to attack) when a shell dropped beside where the Major and I were sleeping. My pillows, boots, leggings, even cheque book were riddled with holes. Fortunately I wasn't there, having just got up, but the Major got off very lightly with only a piece through his shoulder and his left arm fractured. He was delighted too. I offered him £100 for his wounds. But he said he wouldn't sell them for £1000.

At that time it looked as if none of us would ever get through the winter, at all events as lightly as that. We had six men wounded that morning but reinforcements came up next day and eventually we attacked. His infantry would not fight, as usual, except his machine gunners, and we got some of his guns, of which he had a great many of this front. When we attacked Le Quesnoy, it was another nasty battle and we had another wait for a week while the roads were being mended and ammunition and heavy guns were being brought up. I was with a forward section short of the railway in front of Beaudignies, and here again we were shelled continually. I put my detachments into the cellar of a ruined house, and lived in another cellar myself.

One night there were three direct hits on

the house I was in with the signallers – two gas shells and one high explosive. The latter burst on the steps of the cellar. It really seemed as if the end of all things had come. But when we picked ourselves up no damage had been done. The first day we took up this position, when I was looking for somewhere to sleep, a shell whizzed by and hit a house over the road, and a great piece of something hit me flat in the back. Fortunately it was quite flat and not a jagged end, as it left only a bruise and a slight stiffness. I got slightly gassed with two direct gas shells in the house, so we had to go down to the wagon lines.

Three days later the battle for Le Quesnoy took place. He had a lot of guns again there and gave us a bad time. The whole 211 Brigade were in action in an orchard. He shelled us the whole time we were firing the barrage but this battery got off very well though the howitzer battery on the left of the orchard had a dreadful time, being retaliated on continually with eight-inch, simply terrific big shells right in amongst them. Pieces of gun and men were flung all over the orchard. Nine men were killed and all the rest of the howitzer battery were wounded. They went on shooting till the last gun was put out of action and two of their officers were killed and one wounded.

They were all miners from Cumberland – a fine magnificent stamp of man.

We had to advance while the barrage was still going on and the battle raging like billy-o. I had to bring the gun limbers and all the ammunition wagons right through Beaudignies before it was light in order to get them to their new position over the Le Quesnoy railway to shoot the next barrage and support the infantry. Shells seemed to be bursting in every street and house of this horrible village, and all the cottages with thatched roofs were burning like bonfires. I didn't think I would ever get all these men and horses through. I imagined direct hits on the leading teams which would block the way for all the rest. However, we got through all right – only a few horses being slightly wounded that whole day.

In the middle of this village by the church there were some crossroads and we found some infantry transport who had lost their way. They were quietly sitting wondering which way to go amidst all this infernal din and hell let loose. How wonderful it must be to have no imagination. I am sure people who are not frightened on occasions like this can have absolutely none at all.

The New Zealanders did awfully well the Le Quesnoy day, as the Germans meant to hold us up, and everyone was to stand and fight. The German machine gunners did stand and killed a lot of our infantry and the 63rd Division, who are the Artists Rifles, had all crawled and formed little bunches and died in small parties. Some of them were still sitting up and bandaging themselves when they got it. One goes up to them to see if one can help them at all and finds they are dead. Battlefields are a ghastly sight, especially at night when the ghastly white faces stare up at you.

This is all very lugubrious, but it's all over now so it doesn't matter talking about it as there is no need to worry any more. The fighting since August had not been a walkover by any means. According to most people who have been out here for some time, it has been the hardest fighting of the whole war, because it has been so continuous and the Germans have fought their artillery so well – also their machine gunners. They were always killed but they fought their guns till the last and then put up their hands. They looked so surprised and terrified when they realised they were not going to be taken prisoners.

We are going to Germany for a few days now. I think the 42nd Division are going to occupy Koblenz. It really doesn't look as if we are going to be released for some time, but of course someone has got to occupy the Rhine districts.

I must close now as the mail is just going. I hope Father is keeping fit and well and is allowed enough coal to keep himself warm!! Very best love to Father and your dear old self, and all at home.

Your ever affec son,

Douglas

PS Please thank Aunty Kittie so much for the socks. They've just arrived and are exceedingly welcome as several pairs have disappeared in the mud of last month.

Derek Malcolm's christening, 1932, St Paul's, Knightsbridge. Father (extreme left) and mother (second from right) well apart.

What my father didn't mention was the fact that he was awarded the Military Cross for conspicuous courage and devotion to duty on 20 October, 1918. The citation reads,

> While acting as Artillery FOO he spent 36 hours with the advanced Infantry establishing OPs and making visits to the various Company Commanders under very heavy shell and MG fire. He sent back information which was of the highest value, and although he knew he could be relieved he refused to leave the advanced Infantry until the line had been consolidated.

It was signed by the major-general, commanding the 42nd Division.

PART III

Yelvertoft Manor in the late twenties.

CHAPTER 10
BETWEEN THE WARS

By the time the war ended, there had been a hint of reconciliation, suggested by my mother's visit to my father during the course of the trial. Officially they lived together, but in fact spent much of the time apart. There was a flat in London, first at Cadogan Square and then, when that was sold, in Charles Street.

There was also a country house in Northamptonshire called Yelvertoft Manor, bought around 1922. My mother was in London for much of the time, while my father remained in the manor house where there were stables from which he could choose his mounts and hunt with the Pytchley. At one time, there were fourteen horse boxes at Yelvertoft and six grooms. Much to my father's annoyance, since it proved almost as costly as the horses and grooms, my mother added a laundry, staffed by locals. Seven resident servants looked after the two occupants who entertained regularly, with guests usually invited by my more socially inclined mother.

She was not much enamoured of chasing foxes, though she rode handily side-saddle, as was the custom for women in those days, and hunted with my father from time to time. She preferred to receive guests back in the house, most of them from London. The then Duke of Windsor, later the abdicating King Edward, visited once. My father told me many years later that the Duke wasn't much good on a horse, and likely to fall off and harm himself by taking too many risks jumping while out hunting. He said all hell would break loose if it happened while the Duke was being entertained at Yelvertoft and in all probability he would have to take the blame for allowing it.

My father adored the hunt, going out several times a week and writing a regular diary which, if you were not a hunting man, might persuade you against the pursuit of the fox for life, not so much for the cruelty as the boredom.

> Heythrop, Wednesday, 30 September, New Barn – Rode Infatuation and hunted all round Sherborne. One brace accounted for, I think. The mare was very interested and behaved perfectly. She is a lovely ride. There is no ride like a blood horse.

> Heythrop, Friday, 9 October, Shipton Manor – Derek came to the meet with Nanny Potter. He's now five. I've no desire to see him bloodied unless he wants it. A nice little hunt ensued. Rode Endeavour again. The mare jumped a few stone walls very well but hit one and got a little poisoning in her near fire joint. It's no use. She must be sold.

Heythrop, Saturday, 28 November, Taynton – Rode Endeavour. Nothing like as good as Infatuation, but a decent jumper. Such a bad day. No use writing anything about it. Plenty of foxes but we had the worst huntsman in the world. Hopeless.

Heythrop, Friday, 18 December, Moreton-in-the-Marsh – Ten miles in pouring rain – wet through when I arrived at the meet – should have worn a mackintosh. A goodish hunt in the morning round the Swells and Slaughters.

North Warwick Hunt Ball. Douglas Malcolm with monocle, second from right, front row. Dorothy Malcolm, first right, back row.

Finished up near Bourton-on-the-Water. Rode the big horse again. A bit of a sticky jumper. Needs winding up. The rascal kicked out at another horse – gave him a hiding which fairly set him alight. No proper scent.

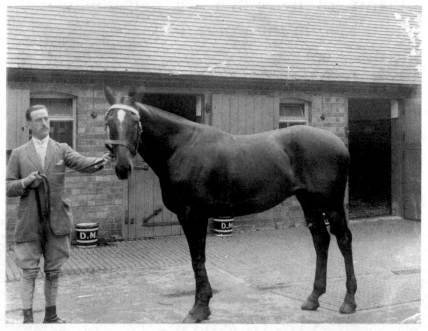

Douglas Malcolm at Yelverton, c. 1925.

This was his life and London society didn't appeal to him at all. At heart he was a countryman but allowed my mother to pursue her friends there while he pursued the foxes. He used to tell me he didn't much care for the kill. It was the riding over country which gave him the satisfaction. There seemed to be a tacit arrangement between my parents that they went their own ways. Perhaps he had found someone else, though I doubt it. There was never the hint of a mistress. My mother, though, was soon surrounded by male admirers once again. Among them were George Robey, the legendary music hall comedian, the painter Augustus John, the conductor Toscanini, who had once offered to train her voice, the Hegelian philosopher Geoffrey Muir and the well-known producer Nigel Playfair, for whom she performed in the lead as *The Duchess of Malfi* at Oxford under her stage name of Sonia Seton. She used that name, she said, because it wasn't done to perform under one's husband's name.

A letter dated June 1926, from George Robey, suggests that his friendship with my mother may not have been entirely platonic. But I have my doubts as to the sexual nature of many of her conquests. Admiration was what she wanted, even adoration. The bedroom had got her into too much trouble before. Robey's letter read,

Dorothy Malcolm at Yelverton, c. 1925.

My darling, lovely Dorothy,

It is hell, but I am once again going on tour and so shall not be able to see you for fully three months. Forgive me, but you know I have to do it. It is my living. But your presence will remain with me throughout the often dreary business of going from one place to another entertaining the populace as best I can. You tell me I am funny and that my voice is good too. I hope you are right. But my voice is nothing to yours.

Sometimes I doubt that the celebrity I have attained is worth the life I have to lead. I would like to be with you always, with nobody recognising either of us. But, alas, it is not possible. When I reach London again, I shall immediately get in touch. But I will be careful, I promise you. Nothing will ever be done to compromise you or to inflict myself upon you further than is wise and honourable. Be sure, though, that my thoughts remain with you, and your beauty and good nature remain securely fastened to my heart.

With love and admiration,
George

There was also a letter, written many years later, from Geoffrey Muir, which I discovered among my mother's papers, telling her how difficult it was to get me into Merton College, Oxford, of which he was Warden. There were candidates of rather more academic and/or athletic prowess to consider. In fact, of some 125 hopefuls, only nineteen were to be accepted and it was doubtful that I deserved to be one of the chosen few.

Dorothy Malcolm with horse and dogs at Yelvertoft.

At my interview I was asked not about my exam results but about whether I wished to be a wet or dry bob should I enter the college. This meant whether I wished to play cricket or to row during the summer term. You could not do both. I had

219

done my research well enough to know that the Merton crew was at that time one of the best at the university, at or near the Head of the River during the early fifties and exceedingly proud of it. 'Wet bob,' I replied, even though it was patently obvious that, at around five foot six and barely nine stone in weight, I had little hope of becoming an oarsman of any note. Little did they know that I could hardly swim, despite my long sojourn at Bexhill-on-Sea. What they wanted, I discovered, was someone small and light who might be prevailed upon to become a cox – not an occupation to cherish since you were invariably blamed for bad steering if the crew lost and dumped unceremoniously into the water if they managed to win. When asked if I had any experience of coxing, I replied in the affirmative. It seemed to help. But the Warden's insistence that I be considered seriously for a place at Merton aided my cause even more. His letter to my mother read as follows,

O Seraph,
How lovely to hear from you again after all this time, and how wonderful it would be to actually see you. Yes, I will do everything I can for Derek. I'm so sorry he could not manage to get into Magdalen. We will certainly see what we can do for him at Merton. But it will be difficult. His exam results are no more than average and there

are many who would seem to have a better chance than he. He must come up here and do his viva voce and we will see whether we can squeeze him in. I much look forward to seeing him, and soon you. I am married now, so we must be just old friends. I assure you I will do everything in my power to help. So many loving memories, Seraph.

Your

Geoffrey

Having been incarcerated in select boarding schools since the age of four, I took to the comparative freedom of university life with some enthusiasm – too much, in fact. I revelled, like a good many others, in new friendships with a wide circle of the kind of young men, and women, I had never met before. I joined various societies, including the Film Society, OUDS (the drama society) and played tennis, squash and cricket for Merton. This would have surprised Parr, my deprecating Eton housemaster, who thought I wasn't much good at anything. My greatest distinction in squash was to play three consecutive matches for the College on the same afternoon when two other members of the Merton team failed to turn up – I won them all, which would have surprised Parr even more. The third match was with a rather portly young man who told me he was just there to make up the team and had only played the game once before. He turned out to be Colin Cowdrey, who was later to become the England cricket captain and one of the finest batsmen of the post-war era. I won the first game 9–1, and the second 9–5, whereupon miraculously he divined how to play the game properly, took the next two 10–8 and 9–7 but finally lost the last one 8–10. Considering his inexperience, his girth and his lack of pace, this was a remarkable achievement. Like all great sportsmen, he had an amazingly fast eye. He could pick up the ball and place it accurately far quicker than most. Had he taken me on again, he would undoubtedly have won.

My best memory of cricket was scoring 99 not out against the University Women's team. I was, however, dropped four times and took so long about it that my captain declared, specifically, he said, to stop me flirting with the wicketkeeper.

Otherwise, I spent endless late evenings discussing life with my own particular circle of fellow students and putting off work until the last possible moment, which was generally too late. Not surprisingly, the essays I read to my tutor were adjudged poor to moderate. My parents seldom visited during term and rarely together. When they did come, I was fearful of introducing them to my new friends unless they came from public schools. A few of them did, but not many. At Merton, even in those days, the public school boys were vastly out-numbered by those who came from state schools.

I loved both my parents, as they undoubtedly loved me. But I did not love what they had come to represent. They seemed to be living in a world whose values I no longer recognised. I could talk to them about very little without straining to avoid an argument. I had no intention of cutting myself off from them. But I was now living a new and exciting life, and their own seemed sadly irrelevant. I do not know whether my mother, on her visits, also saw Geoffrey Muir privately. But she did so only once with me. On that occasion Muir was also entertaining Sir Thomas Beecham, the great conductor, now an old man, before a concert of his at the Sheldonian. Muir, his wife and my mother and I were chatting in the hallway of the Warden's Lodgings, waiting for the great man to come downstairs when there was an almighty noise, like a series of heavy bumps. Looking up, we saw Beecham hurtling down, arriving at the base of the stairway in a heap, having apparently lost his footing at the top. Rushing to his aid, the Warden and I helped him first to his feet and then to a stiff drink. He seemed none the worse for wear, only commenting, when he had caught his breath, 'I have done some odd things in my time. But never have I fallen quite so far, quite so fast.' He had to be helped on to the concert platform by the leader of his orchestra, the Royal Philharmonic, that night. But, as usual, he gave a magnificent concert, finishing with a superb performance of Goldmark's often disparaged

Rustic Wedding Symphony and followed this with a speech, which had the packed audience of undergraduates roaring with laughter. At the very end he was helped off again, grimacing visibly, to a standing ovation.

Though I had very little in the way of a relationship with either the Warden or my own tutor, I and a few others did have a rather strange intimacy with one of the older dons, who was virtually retired but still living in rooms at the college. He would invite us to tea frequently, perhaps wishing to keep in contact with the new generation of undergraduates. He used to leave us notes in our pigeon-holes at the Lodge by the main entrance to the College. I'll always remember one of them. It simply read, 'Sunday 4 p.m. Come to tea – cream buns and mescalin.' He knew of my fondness for cream buns, though not that Laurel and Hardy had given me a special taste for them. But mescalin? I doubt if any don now would pen such a note, substituting LSD or E for mescalin. But when I went to tea, I was a trifle worried as to whether the cream buns contained some substance that would make us attempt to fly out of the window. Nothing untoward happened, however, nor did anyone behave as if they had taken anything more than too much sugar. Probably just as well, since most of my circle, including myself, were only into alcohol. No one I know did drugs. Not even pot. That time was to come. Then, it was advisable not to drink too much Tio Pepe sherry before dinner in Hall in case one sat next to one of the dons.

The elderly professor who invited me to tea so regularly had a sense of humour I much appreciated, especially when it came to celebrating my twenty-first birthday. He knew I liked Dylan Thomas and sent me a book of poetry by the alcoholic but eloquent Welsh poet. Inside the cover he wrote, 'On the best of days, the worst of poets.'

I must have been an appalling student to teach, reading out essays with very little original thought in them, largely cribbed wholesale from books. I was reading History, having gone up to Merton to read English but being totally put off by the prospect of grinding through Anglo-Saxon and not being able to study any literature penned after the nineteenth century.

We were abjured to read, learn and inwardly digest Aristotle, taught at Merton by a don whose wife was a fairly well-known and beautiful continental film star. This intrigued us all greatly, since he looked like the back of a bus and none of us could understand what she saw in him. I remember him giving a lecture to our group on Aristotle's *Politics* and asking me a question I was totally unable to answer. 'Malcolm,' he said, 'Have you even read Aristotle's *Politics*?' 'No,' I heard myself reply, 'but I've seen the film.'

Fortunately, he had a sense of humour. 'Yes,' he said, 'so have I. But, alas, there was no part for my wife.' He was not averse to occasional ribbing. But when his wife came to Oxford for an official Merton occasion, she looked at us all with some disdain and refused to sign autographs.

The people I remember with the greatest affection from my days of living at College – you were boarded out in 'digs' after the first year – were the college servants, or 'scouts'. We relied upon them not only to keep our rooms clean and reasonably tidy but also to cover up any misdemeanours, like girls in the rooms after hours, or rowdy drinking sessions. Mine was called George, who was careful to note which football and cricket team I supported. He would present me with my early morning cup of tea on match days with the words, 'Good morning, sir – Brighton and Hove Albion 2, Watford 1, or Sussex 347 for 8 declared, Somerset 40 for 1.'

Nemesis, for me, was inevitable. And it came sooner rather than later. I failed part of my preliminary exams at the end of the first year and compounded it by attempting to smuggle a girl from St Hilda's College over Merton College walls. It was late at night and there were spikes on top of the wall. With the girl perched precariously on the spikes, I tried to lever her up to the top and, in doing so, fell backwards into the college gardens. I landed straight in the path of the Warden himself who was walking his dog before retiring for the night. I remember the look of acute horror on his face when he saw it was me. What on earth was he going to tell Seraph? Considering I had also failed my Prelims, there was nothing for it but to punish me with what was then known as rustication, which meant two terms away from Merton and then a return to face the failed exam again.

My mother was furious. I had let down the very man who had moved heaven and earth to secure a place for an undeserving candidate in his college, and made her thoroughly ashamed. My father was less disturbed, confining himself to the comment, 'Bloody fool – who was the girl?' And to demonstrate that he was not as concerned as my mother, he took me off to the races at Lingfield. Much to my surprise, there was a horse running in the 2.30 called Rustication. I backed it with £2 borrowed from my father. It won at 25–1. The £50 I won almost seemed worth the stain of my disgrace at Merton.

Some twenty years later, I remember visiting Sarah, my present wife, who was then at St Anne's. It was around four in the afternoon and I asked the elderly lady on duty at the Lodge for the number of her room. She told me and then, to my surprise, asked if I was staying the night. No, I said, I'm taking her out to tea. 'Well, you can stay the night if you want,' she said, 'but we don't like you staying for more than three days. It tends to interfere with their work.' After the episode at Merton, I could scarcely believe what I heard.

Gradually things calmed down after my rustication.

Mr Pilcher was called in again, much to his delight, to instruct me and gaze fondly at my mother. I took the exam a second time and passed, returning to Merton, slightly shame-faced but secure in the knowledge that, although I had missed two terms, I would have an extra summer term to study for my degree – or perhaps just to enjoy myself once again with my friends.

It was at about this time that I first met Stanley. We were both members of the tennis club at Cooden Beach, near Bexhill. He was some twenty years older than me and worked for Shell. Out of his baggy tennis shorts, he invariably wore a dark suit and acted exactly like the respectable businessman he was. I noticed he drank rather a lot of gin and tonics at the bar where, even if there was a crowd, he could get himself instantly served. His voice was deep and throaty and seemed to attract the attention of any barman at once. He chainsmoked cigarettes but, despite his weight, was a good player with whom I soon formed a regular partnership. I was not as strong, but he liked playing with me, he said, because I made him laugh by swearing at myself loudly when missing a shot or making a mistake. He would never have done any such thing himself.

One evening during that summer, he suggested we went for a drink in Bexhill and then for a walk along the Promenade. It started to rain so we sat alone in a shelter smoking and talking. What happened next totally surprised me. He suddenly put his arms around me and pressed his face up against mine. And as I got up to get away from his embrace, he pressed himself against me. I shouted for him to stop and he instantly did. I was both shocked and angry, and told him that, if he ever touched me again, I would cease to see him. He seemed mortified. He apologised profusely, promised never to make such a move again and said that he hoped we could continue play tennis together. We walked home in silence, not knowing what to say to each other. But when I saw him at the tennis club the next weekend, he took me aside and said: 'Let's continue to be friends. Rest assured I will never bother you again.'

Part of the shock of this embarrassing incident was undoubtedly caused by the fact that Stanley had seemed so straight and normal. No one would have suspected him of homosexuality for an instant and, although I now know there are many gay people like that, as a young man I thought I could tell who was homosexual and who was not pretty easily. I later discovered, through talking to Stanley, that his elaborate mask of jolly normality, during which he would sometimes pass appreciative comments to me about some of the more attractive girls at the tennis club, had slipped for the first time in his life when he had made his clumsy pass at me.

He apologised again and again for the incident and begged me to forget it. I said I would, but wondered whether it might not be better if I broke off my relationship with him straightaway. My instinct was that it would. But, at this vulnerable juncture in my life, I needed a friend and he seemed to be there for me. We began to talk about our lives, generally in the farthest corner of some bar or other where he would consume several large gins and smoked constantly while I toyed with a half pint of beer.

I told him of my odd home and moaned about having to stay in Bexhill while I was rusticated. He was a highly sympathetic listener. When he told me about his own circumstances, I realised that he was indeed an unhappy man. He hated working for Shell and wanted to leave as soon as possible. He had few real friends there and relatives who had no idea of his sexual orientation and could certainly not be told of it. Women, he said, had tried to get near to him but, although some of them would have made him a good wife, he had brushed them away. I realised he was, despite his social abilities, which seemed to make everyone like him as 'good old Stanley', a very lonely man. What I didn't realise was that he was falling in love with me.

He only confessed that in one of his many letters to me later. At first it just seemed to me that we were very good friends. I needed someone with whom to talk, about things I could never tell my parents or even my friends at Oxford. I put to the back of my mind the thought that he was even more vulnerable than me and that the best thing to do, for him, would have been to end the relationship for good.

When I finally left by train for Oxford again, he was there on the station. So were my parents. But he stood where they couldn't see him and waved me goodbye from another part of the platform. He never wanted to meet by parents even though I occasionally thought it might have been a good idea. A few days later he wrote me a letter. It read,

Old chum,
I was glad I went to the station to say goodbye to you. But I confess it hurt me greatly. I watched the train go into the distance with tears in my eyes. Yes, I know this is silly and I ask you to forgive me for what I am about to write. We are, I hope, good friends. But for me there will always be something more. You know why, and I am desperately sorry to burden you with this. But I must tell you now, and ask you to decide what you wish to do about it. I have never loved anyone in my life before. But I do love you, with all my heart. I know that nothing can ever make you recriprocate and you must rest assured that nothing physical will ever occur again. So can we remain friends? I hope so, because I think you need some support in your life as I do in mine. I hope also that everything will go well back at Merton, and should you wish me to visit you there I will gladly do so

when I can. But if you would rather break our friendship now, please tell me. I will readily understand. But I will miss our tennis together and all the laughs we had on court. You know that I will miss our other meetings too. You are the only person who makes me laugh insanely!

Now to my main news. I intend to offer my resignation to Shell and hope to get enough money off them to get a house somewhere. I don't know where yet but it will be as far away from that world as possible. Keep in touch, unless you don't want to.

Ever,
    Stanley

Stanley, with Jackie, Derek Malcolm's daughter.

I did keep in touch, and we corresponded regularly during term and met as regularly back at Bexhill. Eventually, he did resign from Shell and went to live in Alderney which he said was populated largely by drunks and seagulls. I went to visit him there on several occasions in the small bungalow he rented. He took me to the local pubs where the customers seemed to drink gins and tonic even quicker than he did. Everyone seemed to like him and he played the game of socialising with them with some resolution.

I never lost contact with Stanley as the years went by, since he was the best friend I'd got. When I married in Cheltenham he sent me his congratulations and said he hoped one day to be able to meet my wife. It must have been a bad moment for him. But thereafter he became ever more frank with me, either in letters or in person, about his sexual orientation. He said he was going to try to have an affair before he died but doubted whether he could manage it. The last thing he ever wanted to do was to go to 'cottageing' in public lavatories or even to a gay club. He disliked people he considered to flaunt their gayness openly.

One of his last letters to me was one of triumph. But it seemed very sad to me.

Old chum,
    Hope married life suits you. She seems a very nice girl and I look forward to meeting

233

her. Life goes on as usual at Alderney. Not much tennis, too much drinking. Conversation nil. But I have to announce a slightly comic victory. At the age of 67, I have finally had my first sex! It was with a friendly milkman who came to my door to deliver my pint and was persuaded in for a cup of tea. I won't go into the sordid details, except to say that we didn't manage much, largely because it is too late for me. He asked to see me again, and wants to introduce me to his father. Maybe we will become friends. Goodness knows what will transpire, or even whether I really want anything more to happen. But at least – and at last – I can say my virginity has been partially displaced by experience, if that's the right word for it. Life is quite extraordinary, isn't it? Do write soon, old chum.

Ever,
    Stanley

Not long afterwards, a female friend of his wrote to me, telling me Stanley had cancer of the lungs and was going to hospital in England for treatment. I wrote to him immediately and I found him in a private room in a clinic near Hastings. He was obviously very ill and we could only talk for a few minutes. I think he knew he was dying but refused to talk about himself and kept asking how I was getting on. He was still smoking despite the tut-tutting of the nurses. It was a dark, rainy day in winter and I had to get back to London. My wife was waiting for me in the car and, though she had never met Stanley and had refused to come into the clinic, she cried when I told her of his condition.

I had the feeling that I would never see him again and I didn't. He died a week later.

We hadn't seen each other very much in his last years but I missed his weekly letters, always asking about me and seldom telling me much about himself. He was the best of friends but I never stopped feeling guilty about his real feelings for me and wondering whether it would have been easier for him if I'd never existed. It is difficult even to imagine now, in these much easier days for gay people, what a shrouded and unhappy life he had. And I wondered, when I went to his funeral, where a few of his friends had gathered, how many of those present knew of his true nature. I looked around but couldn't see anyone who looked like a milkman. But as I left the crematorium, a youngish man arrived in an old and battered car. 'Have I missed Stanley's funeral?' he said. He looked crestfallen when I said he had and drove off again.

When I returned to Merton after my rustication, I behaved much as I had before, almost as if I had no intention of heeding the warning. I played even more tennis and squash, talked even deeper into the night and worked on my essays in an even more desultory fashion, almost never attending the appropriate lectures.

I also acted, appearing for the famous producer Neville Coghill as the Clown in *All's Well That Ends Well*, not one of Shakespeare's very finest parts or plays. Coghill stopped me once at rehearsals and said, 'Malcolm, I wonder if you could play the Clown as Buster Keaton?'

'No,' I said. 'I can't manage that. But what about Oliver Hardy or Stan Laurel?'

'Oh, very well then,' he replied, 'but I think it will have to be Laurel in your case. Laurel it was, although I added a few of Hardy's double takes for good measure. I managed to get a lot of laughs from the audience that way, but would have traded them for a good notice from Kenneth Tynan, who came down to review the production. He did not oblige, writing 'Derek Malcolm as the Clown seemed to have strayed from an undergraduate review.' I did, however, get a better mention from Harold Hobson in the *Sunday Times*. He wrote, 'Derek Malcolm not only sang his song well, but provided a Clown who for once was appropriately funny.'

That song was a problem for me. I spent hours trying to remember it and even longer attempting to sing it.

> *Was this fair face the cause, quoth she,*
> *Why the Grecians sacked Troy?*
> *Fond done, fond done,*

Was this King Priam's joy?
With that she sighed as she stood,
With that she sighed as she stood,
And gave this sentence then,
Among nine bad if one be good,
Among nine bad if one be good,
There's yet one good in ten.

I tried it out on my mother several times and she sang it superbly. I couldn't compete. But my father had some more useful advice. 'Now, look here,' he said, 'just speak it first and then hum it and then sing it softly. When you've done that, bawl it out as loud as you can. Pretend you're singing it on parade.' I did what he said, and it worked, for Harold Hobson at least. But not, unfortunately, for Kenneth Tynan, whom everyone was desperately anxious to impress.

CHAPTER 11

GOODBYE, DORRIE DEAR

Having secured my place at Merton through influence, I was given my first job in journalism through the good offices of Etienne Bellenger, who knew someone influential at the now defunct *Daily Sketch*. I was expected to go to nightclubs and spy on the glitterati. In those days they were not footballers or pop stars but young bloods from the aristocracy who might or might not be having affairs with each other. The job was a complete pain and I was given it because it was thought that, as an Old Etonian, I was almost certain to know the people who would figure in the gossip columns of the day. Actually, I did not have much interest in any of these people, but managed to invent one or two stories that satisfied my editor if not those who figured, often somewhat inaccurately, in them.

The business of chasing aristos round places like the Edmundo Ros Club at dead of night reminded me rather of the school roll-call at Eton where those without titles came at the bottom of the list thus:

Prince Bulawayo? – yes, sir
The Duke of Kent? – yes, sir
Lord Chester? – yes, sir
Sir Ian Dunstan? – yes, sir
The Honourable Charles Ogilvy? –
   yes, sir
Malcolm? – yes, sir

I was not very good as a gossip writer and it was soon decided that I would be better off in Cheltenham on the local paper owned by the group. After all, Cheltenham Races, the premier National Hunt meeting, would surely be of interest to someone like myself. There I began my career as a journalist proper, ringing up the Cotswold fire stations, ambulance, hospital and police services each day to find out about car crashes, fires and the like.

The chief reporter was a veteran called Mr Hurford who conducted the day's operations peering at us over his glasses from the top of the long reporters' table. His main objective was to keep out of trouble. By now, however, he had lost his capacity to convince the editor that he knew when news was news. One day the police reported that a plane had crashed near Cheltenham, killing the pilot and his passenger. It was obviously the big story of the moment, but Mr Hurford, knowing the editor was a Mason, favoured instead the large Masonic funeral of one of the town's well-known councillors. This incensed the editor who, although an inveterate snob, realised that a plane crash had more news value than a funeral. Storming into the reporters' room, he said to Hurford, 'I want the crash as a lead story. Take Malcolm off the funeral and put him on to it!'

With words that went down at the office like some kind of epitaph, Hurford mumbled, 'But, sir, it was only a little plane . . .'

I also worked as a court reporter where I observed humans every bit as eccentric as my parents, some possibly more so. The very first case I reported concerned a man from the neighbouring town of Gloucester who had apparently had sexual congress with a pig at a farm near Cheltenham. The police evidence, read out in the usual matter-of-fact tones, quoted the defendant as saying, 'I went into the farmyard to steal a chicken and to seduce a pig, as I hadn't had a woman for months.'

Not a glimmer of a smile lit up the stern face of the magistrate as he told the defendant, 'You will be fined £30. We don't like this sort of thing in Cheltenham. Go back to Gloucester. And stay there.'

I was paid £4 a week to hear these and other strange revelations emanating from the Cotswolds on behalf of the *Gloucestershire Echo* and my father sent me £2 a week to supplement my slim income. However poor I was, it was better than sitting in nightclubs until two in the morning trying to find out whether it was Lady Agatha or the Hon. Miss

Helena at the next table talking intimately with Lord Fitzpatrick.

I eventually got in trouble with the police twice myself, once appearing in court as a defendant. The first brush with the law came when I was charged with careless driving as a learner driver. I had not only failed to be driving with a licence holder accompanying me but had neglected to stop at a junction, and hit a van, overturning it and slightly injuring its driver. This was hardly a minor infringement of the driving code and I hired a solicitor who told me to appear in court with my Old Etonian tie and apologise as humbly as I could. It worked like a charm. I was told to drive more carefully in future and fined a paltry £4. I think the presiding magistrate recognised the tie.

On the second occasion I was taken off to the police cells after being apprehended getting out of my car near my digs at around midnight. The officer asked me if I owned the car, which was a smart-looking if second-hand MGM. He thought I'd stolen it and was certain when I was totally unable to remember its number plate. He was irritated further by my remark that it was perhaps unwise but not illegal to be vague. The editor had to come personally to the cells to vouch for me at 2.30 a.m. He was not best pleased.

On Saturdays, I was frequently sent to report on the rugby matches at Cheltenham College. My first task was to go into the changing rooms and get the teams from the opposing captains. Being merely the local reporter and not a member of the national press, who occasionally came down to report the matches, I was generally received with scant attention until, one afternoon, I decided again to wear my Old Etonian tie. This instantly produced results and the teams were spelt out to me with alacrity.

I eventually had my revenge on the editor for making me attend so many rain-soaked matches and all those Masonic funerals. I was in charge of the Letters column at the time and, knowing the editor was extremely fond of cricket, decided to lead with a letter from one Bert Williams, who persistently wrote to the *Echo* on the subject. This time, he was extolling the virtues of the Gloucestershire batsman Jack Crapp, who had just scored a century against the touring Australians during Cheltenham Cricket Week. Crapp, he wrote, was a good enough player to be included in the England team and his latest innings proved it. The editor was delighted and said the letter should be used at the top of the page. Much to the glee of the other reporters, I managed to get the headline across four columns through all three editions: WE MUST ALL TAKE OUR HATS OFF TO CRAPP.

When I got married for the first time, during my years on the *Gloucestershire Echo*, both my parents came to the wedding, having smartened themselves up for the occasion. But my mother was no longer the woman she had once been. I cannot remember now when her mental state first started to deteriorate; nor how my father and I first became aware that something was wrong. But at the wedding, now well in never-never land, she asked my prospective in-laws, 'Who is that pretty girl with Derek?' This was the girl who was about to become my wife. They had no idea of my mother's condition, since she was still a beautiful, intelligent-looking woman and capable of being charming to everyone, even when she had little notion of who they were or even where she was.

She spent the last years of her life in a fog of incomprehension, eating very little since neither she nor my father was now capable of cooking anything but porridge or boiled eggs. And their new home, a ground-floor flat in a shabby Victorian block near the Promenade, to which they had been forced to move when 2 Channel View proved too much for them, soon became a mirror image of the last one. I visited occasionally, though not with my wife, since there was no room and I had to sleep once again on the sofa in the sitting room.

It was on one of those sad and increasingly rare visits, which I had come to dread, that she died in her bed of a stroke in the middle of the night. She had suffered from high blood pressure for some time and couldn't always remember to take her medicine. I heard her cry out in the early hours of the morning, but she was unconscious when I went into her bedroom with my father. We rang for the ambulance but, when it arrived, she was dead. They left her there on the bed until the morning and, before the undertakers called, my father kissed her on the forehead and said, 'Goodbye, Dorrie dear, goodbye. We've been through a lot together, haven't we?' He must have been remembering a whole lifetime of regrets.

I couldn't bear to bid her one last farewell but, after her body was taken away, went for a walk past Bexhill's famous De La Warr Pavilion, where she often used to go to hear the salon orchestra at teatime. They were playing a selection from the Ivor Novello shows she loved so much and, as if on cue, launched into 'Some Day My Heart Will Awake', one of her favourite songs. That's when the numbness of loss vanished and the bleak reality of her death really hit me. I cried all the way back home, remembering someone who had enormous personal warmth, an infinite capacity, when she wanted, to make you feel loved and a mischievous sense of humour that seemed to coincide exactly with mine. I also thought of her frustrating life, once so full of promise but latterly something like a living hell. We had not seen each other much and the once regular letters from her, sometimes including a pound note or two to supplement my income, had long since ceased. But I thought of her better days and the performances we had put on for each other, laughing so much that tears used to course down our cheeks.

Not long afterwards my father, having sold off what was left of the silver after Manners and family had decamped with their stash years before, decided he'd have to leave the flat. It was a ghastly process. As soon as anyone elderly died in the vicinity, dealers from Brighton would arrive at the door to scavenge for bargains, often persuading the confused and elderly bereaved to part with antiques at totally unrealistic prices. I stopped several of them before they could do too much damage but remember one man, whom my father had unwisely let in, picking up a silver Georgian salt cellar and scrunching it up in his hands. 'There,' he said, 'you can see it's a fake. I'll give you £1 for the metal.' I lost my temper and told him to get out of the flat before I hit him.

My mother was buried at Bexhill Cemetery. Father and I were joined by my aunts Phyllis and Ida. A few of her friends turned up as well, but it was a small affair which didn't so much comfort the living as simply dump the dead. My father never returned to the grave and, to my shame, nor did I.

Not long after her death, my father left the rented flat and went to live in a country hotel called Moor Hall near Ninfield, a few miles from Bexhill, where there was a stables, a large garden and the *Daily Telegraph* came automatically to the guests at breakfast. He was still well-off by average standards but felt himself to be a pauper, having succeeded in losing the riches of his youth without having had the luxury of enjoying them much. The hotel was owned and run by a very smooth and sophisticated Austrian who was tolerant of the eccentricities of my father, provided they didn't interfere too much with the equilibrium of the other guests. He could no longer go bathing in his underpants, but was wont to scuttle along in them to the nearest bathroom to the consternation of the guests who didn't know him. 'Oh, it's only the Captain,' the proprietor would say, 'He's perfectly harmless.' He was one of the few permanent occupants of Moor Hall and was regarded fondly by the staff as a kind of talisman of earlier times who was almost part of the furniture. Though now in his late seventies, he kept himself fit enough to go hunting with the East Sussex, and he still played bridge and golf. He added another sport to his list by becoming a croquet player of some cunning.

Douglas Malcolm at Moor Hall in 1965 – a dab hand at croquet.

By now I had a daughter by my first wife and visited him with her. He liked Jackie and remarked that my wife had 'a decent pair of legs', which was tantamount to saying I had made a good choice. He and I played croquet together, forming a partnership very few could beat. Cheating seemed to be an integral part of the game and we were the local experts. It was a brief interlude in his life during which he was as happy as I had ever seen him. Though he had hardly looked after my mother, she had been a worry to him in her final years since he was never certain what she would do next. If she went for a walk alone, it was by no means certain that she knew the way back home or could even ask someone directions. He seemed relieved that she had finally gone and perhaps, with her, some of his worst memories. Now he was fed properly, kept warm in winter and could pursue his life relatively free from worry. I felt better for him too.

I was still on the *Echo* but itching to leave for a bigger paper, preferably the *Guardian*, which I now read daily as an antidote to my local. Not that you could easily get the paper in the south of England at that time, other than a day late from Manchester – and certainly not at Moor Hall, where it was considered *non grata* because of its supposedly left-wing views. I tried very hard when I visited, but rarely with any success. 'There were no *Guardians* available,' they used to say sniffily, plonking the *Telegraph* down on the breakfast table.

Eventually my dream of getting a job on the

Guardian came true, and I moved to Manchester as a sub-editor in the department run as a fiefdom by Brian Redhead, then the powerful features editor, who hoped to become editor one day but in the end had to be content to partner John Timpson on *Today*, the BBC's early morning programme. I wrote to Redhead out of the blue suggesting a piece on the Cheltenham Literary Festival. He replied that I could write 1000 words on spec and that, if he liked it, he might use it on the arts page. I had not expected this, nor indeed any reply at all, and settled down nervously to write it. My first attempt was terrible, desperately trying to prove how clever I was and how much I knew about literature and the arts. It didn't work and I knew it. A few hours before the piece was due to be delivered to the copytakers, I tore up the typescript. This, I thought, was the end of my progression from first general reporter and then drama critic of the *Gloucestershire Echo* to a post on the *Guardian*. But I decided I had to send something and sat down again to write an entirely different piece. It was rude about the innate conservatism of Cheltenham and ironic about the pretensions of the Literary Festival. It was the kind of reportage that I knew would get me into considerable trouble locally, were it to be printed. So I added a note at the end of the article that I wished to be called Michael Elliston, my middle two names. I did not imagine for one moment that it would be used and assumed it was the end of any wider career in journalism. Even reading it out to the *Guardian*'s copytakers was embarrassing, though I noted with a glimmer of hope that the woman who typed it laughed out loud here and there.

The next day the news editor of the *Echo* rang me up and said, 'Have you seen the *Guardian* today? There's an appalling article about Cheltenham and the Literary Festival on the arts page by someone called Michael Elliston. I want you to show it to the Festival organisers and ask for a comment. And to the mayor too. We'll get some vox pops later. Could you get your piece to us by four this afternoon; 600 words, please.' I rushed to where I had left the *Guardian* and, opening the arts page, found my scurrilous article had been printed in its entirety, and at the top of the page too. But now I had to face, without blushing, the people of whom I had made fun.

Both the organiser of the Festival and the Conservative mayor were appropriately scandalised. 'Typical', said the mayor, 'of a paper which fortunately very few of us read. Most of the writers are Communists, you know, masquerading as Liberals. The best thing to do is to ignore it. You may print my comment if you must.' I did.

A good few people I knew had read the Michael Elliston piece and were much amused by its irreverent tone. 'Sounds a bit like you,' one of them said, 'I think I'll spread the rumour.' Brian Redhead was amused too and wrote me a letter asking, 'Why are you hiding down there? I'll find you a job when I can. But it won't be immediate because there's no vacancy at the moment. Hang on, and I'll get in touch again.'

The suspicion grew in Cheltenham that someone local had written the article, and that it was as likely as not to be me. But I admitted nothing. Weeks and then months went by without a call from Brian Redhead. Finally, I wrote to him again, by this time more in hope than expectation. A week later, I opened two letters – one from Redhead offering me an interview for a job in Features, one from the then chief reporter, offering an interview for a job with him. I felt I had to choose the former.

The interview went reasonably well until it came to the question, 'Where were you educated?' To which I didn't dare reply 'Eton and Oxford' since I imagined Redhead would not exactly jump for joy at the prospect of an Etonian on his determinedly meritocratic staff. So I said, 'At a school near Windsor, and then at Oxford.'

'God,' he said, 'for a moment I thought you were going to say Eton! All right, you can start in Manchester in a month – how much do you expect to be paid?'

'Well', I said nervously, 'I get 21 guineas in Cheltenham.'

'All right,' he said, 'you'll get £1 more here. Is that OK?' It wasn't, but I accepted immediately. Anything to get away from Cheltenham.

When I arrived in Manchester and got to know the people in Features, I admitted to someone I'd been to Eton and Brian Redhead got to know about it. 'Good God,' he said, 'if I'd known I'd never have employed you.' He was only half joking. Years later, after I had been interviewed by him on his programme, I reminded him of this and he denied it. 'No, no. Not at all,' he said, 'I merely suggested that you seemed a trifle more intelligent than your average Etonian, especially those in the Cabinet.'

The job on the *Guardian* involved subbing, designing and occasionally writing for the arts pages, mostly on the theatre but sometimes on the other arts, even a film or two. My father, though he did not much approve of the paper, was beginning to be quite proud of me and told me that I was the only member of the Malcolms who had any intelligence at all. 'Most of them died from drink or syphilis, you know,' he said, which I'm not sure was entirely true. When I moved from Manchester to the *Guardian* offices in London I was asked (when the paper decided that it couldn't be the only paper left not to cover horse racing) to be the racing correspondent until a proper one could be found. No one else on the staff knew the back of a horse from the front, and I had foolishly put on my *curriculum vitae*, that riding horses was one of my hobbies. My father was exceedingly proud, telling me I had a proper job at last. But he used to complain that some of my 'naps' – the tip of the day – cost him money. 'I only read the paper', he said once, 'for your reports and the Country Diary.' He was still a *Telegraph* man through and through. At least the

251

Telegraph never called Lester Piggott 'Lester Piglet', which the *Guardian* did after I'd phoned in one of my reports from Newmarket. This amused my father no end but not me.

Among the friends my father made at Moor Hall was the notorious Dr Bodkin Adams, the alleged Eastbourne murderer of wealthy widows. He had dinner one evening with him and thought him 'rather a good fellow who very decently paid the bill, doubtless with some of the money he had gathered from his widows'. This, he thought, was as good a joke as Piglet for Piggott.

His other friend, with whom he often had a whisky at the bar, was Don Cockell, the former British heavyweight champion, who treated him with the utmost respect and called him 'the Captain' like everyone else. Cockell was retired by then, having fought and lost in six rounds to Rocky Marciano for the World Heavyweight Championship. He was actually a jumped-up light heavyweight of medium size but wide with it and clearly no match for a boxer who was then the best fighter pound for pound in the world. It was a rather extraordinary friendship between my father and him – one upper middle class to his core, the other a working-class Cockney who had made it big. But they got along well, though they never talked about boxing, which Cockell knew a bit about, nor horses, of which my father knew rather a lot.

He stayed at Moor Hall happily but there was one drawback. He was becoming incontinent with old age and the maids, who regarded him very fondly, could no longer disguise the fact that they had to change his bedsheets every day. The Austrian owner decided regretfully that he'd have to go as soon as I could find him another place. I tried desperately to discover a home locally which would look after him but only succeeded in getting him into another, rather lesser hotel in Bexhill-on-Sea. But the same thing happened there – he was wetting the chairs in the lounge as well as his bed and he wouldn't wear the various attachments the doctor suggested that might have helped. Once again, he had to go, and I had another search to make.

Things were getting pretty desperate when we settled eventually on a large house near Hastings where a small Polish man and his exceedingly fat English wife were setting up a nursing home. My father was to be the very first guest and was given the best room. I did not quite trust them but there was nowhere else to turn. It was a big mistake. He was left alone there for months, since the proprietors of the home were unable to finance the operation properly and, after a full year, there were still only three or four elderly occupants. When I visited him during the winter, I found him shivering in a cold room unable to use the meter for the gas fire since he didn't have enough shillings to put into it. I filled up the meter, left him as much change as I could and vowed to find him another place, even though he said he was too old to move again unless it was to join me in my flat in Highgate.

St Helen's Wood Hotel, Hastings –
Douglas Malcolm's residential home.

But I was now divorced from my wife, and would not have been able to look after an old and incontinent man. My work took me out much of the day and often in the evenings too. But I tried to have him up in London the Christmas before he died, since I was now living with another girl who said she would help look after him for a week or so. He wrote his last letter to me with an old-fashioned charm and sweetness that made me realise how much I was going to miss him.

My dearest Derek,
    Don't tell Aunt Phyllis you are living with someone unmarried, otherwise the Pope

and goodness knows who else would be drawn in! You need not tell the local parson that you are not married either, if and when you meet him. Glad you have named your cat Toby after my last horse. I should love to come to you for Christmas week – we can pick up a pheasant at one of the Macfisheries shops. They do them on the spit and they're so much nicer than turkey. Will not forget to bring some money. Have a nicer bed and a warm room now, thanks to you. I'm old and going fast downhill so must stick it out here, I think. The meals are at odd hours, which would not have suited my friend the Commander at Moor Hall. But I miss it a lot. Have told them here I will be away for a week at Christmas. I like your article in today's *Guardian*. You are really very intelligent. I wouldn't have a child if I were you. It might make things complicated. But talking about bastards, they are generally very much 'all there'. William the Conqueror was one and nearly all the present-day aristocracy are – Charles II got very busy. Looking forward a lot to the 23rd. Will you come down in your car?

Love,

Daddy

Despite what he said about staying put, I was still searching for a suitable home for him near me in

London when I was telephoned by the fat lady from Hastings. She told me that my father had been taken ill with pneumonia after going with an old friend to the meet of the local hunt. It had been a cold and rainy day, and he had got very wet. He was in Hastings hospital. Every day, she said, she took him food from her own kitchen because he preferred her cooking to the catering there.

Rushing down from London, I found that she had not been near him, with food or anything else – a fact about which he was extremely glad, since by now he disliked her as much as I did. But his breathing soon became very bad and he asked me to see what the doctors could do about it. They told me that they could give him morphine and oxygen, which would ease his breathing but that the morphine would almost certainly kill him. Seeing him in that condition, I told them to go ahead. The morphine did its work and he became unconscious and died shortly afterwards, his pneumonia complicated by the discovery of cancer of the lung, probably caused by a lifetime of pipe-smoking. He was eighty-six.

Later I wrote to the local authorities about the home and accused the Polish owner and his wife of neglect. A month afterwards, they closed it. I should have complained a good deal earlier. It was a sad end for a man who, like my mother, had lived a life that was largely unfulfilled, although I couldn't imagine how he would ever have filled it properly, even granted a better marriage. He had never done a day's work in his life after leaving the firm of J. R. Malcolm. I think he regretted it, like so much else. But he remained an affectionate father to me and, towards the end of his life, became proud of my 'success'. He was also extraordinarily tolerant of my somewhat unorthodox lifestyle, as his last letter shows.

Travelling to the local crematorium behind the hearse, I saw a man on the pavement raise his hat in respect as the cars went past. As a small boy my father had said to me, 'Always raise your hat when a chimney sweep or a hearse passes. It's the thing to do, you know.' At that moment, I found myself in tears. He had added, 'But when I die, just throw me away in the dustbin. I don't want any fuss. Funerals are too depressing for words.' I asked for his ashes and scattered them myself on the Sussex Downs. He would have appreciated the fact that there were some horses in the field at the time.

A month or so after my father's funeral, I found a postcard that had been pushed through the letterbox of my London flat in Highgate. It was from my aunt Phyllis who had looked after me so well many years earlier. She wrote, 'My darling Derek – Your mother asked me to tell you after Douglas's death that he was not your real father. Your father was the Italian Ambassador to London who is now also dead. I do not know his name – All my love, Phyllis.'

I suppose I should either have been incredulous, or shocked, or both. But I was neither, although I did wonder what possessed Phyllis to communicate such potentially devastating news on a postcard rather than in a sealed envelope. I still have no idea whether it is true or not, and do not much care either way. I had grown very fond of the father I had known all my life and who, in his stumbling, often uncomprehending manner, had looked after me as best he could. Did he suspect that I might not be his son? If he did, then my admiration for him increases and I have even fonder memories of him. Curiously, I have never been the least bit intrigued about the man my aunt referred to, though I know many would have been. I didn't even bother to look up the records at the time and I never have since. For me, my possibly fake father was my true parent and will always remain so. I never replied to my aunt and she did not refer to it again. But I do remember once, when I was about ten, saying to my mother that I had the same colour eyes as my father. And I also remember her laughing in a way that suggested what I'd said was rather pathetic. It seemed to me even then that she knew something she was not going to tell me.

My aunt Phyllis died a year or two later in a nursing home in Kent. She was a devout Catholic, as my father had intimated in his last letter, and went to meet her maker in a strange way. A nurse came in with her bedtime Ovaltine and said, 'See you in the morning.'

'No you won't,' she said. 'I'm off to God tonight.' She was found dead in her bed the next morning.

She wouldn't deliberately have lied about my parentage, though whether the information on the postcard was accurate I'll never know since Aunt Phyllis frequently tended to get her facts wrong. But when I told the story to a good Italian friend of mine, he checked the records and sent me a photograph of the famous Count Ciano. He was not the Ambassador, he said, but he came to London at the time as Mussolini's emissary. 'You look awfully like him,' he said when we next met. If it was Ciano, I may well not be the only half-Italian bastard he spawned. He is described in Ray Moseley's book *Mussolini's Shadow* as a man who had the sexual appetite of a satyr and, before one trip abroad, had telegraphed the local Italian consul-general, 'Provide women.' He was eventually executed by Mussolini as a conspirator against him. Quite possibly my father was somebody else at the Italian embassy. There is an old photograph left by my mother which seems to come from that period with a name written on it with a surname that is indecipherable but with the Christian name 'Nanni'. I have no means of knowing whether this was just another of my mother's conquests or genuinely the man who was my father. The inscription reads, in English, 'To my darling.' The mystery will never be solved and I have no desire for it to be.

A few years after my father's death, I was offered the post of film critic of the *Guardian*, which I held for some thirty years. Moving from sub-editing to horse racing and then to the cinema may seem an odd progress. But in those days it was not so peculiar. The *Guardian* had a tradition of its writers being all-rounders. The great Neville Cardus wrote on cricket and classical music with equal distinction. I should know. I subbed much of his copy, which used to be brought to my desk by his chauffeur, since I was the only one who could be relied upon to read his writing – he couldn't type. I didn't deal with his cricket reports, but would get his concert notices in not one but two stages. The first was a long and learned dissertation on the main work of the night. This was delivered before the concert. The second was a paragraph to put at the beginning, and another to place at the end. The opening paragraph was something like, 'At the Royal Festival Hall last night, Herbert von Karajan and the Berlin Philharmonic played Mahler's Third Symphony.' Then I had to insert the discussion of the piece before the final paragraph, which would be a short critique of how it was actually played – 'Mr Karajan imposed himself upon the Symphony with considerable élan but also some thought, though one did not always feel quite enough of the piece's internal drama. His orchestra responded with the conviction that was clearly born of a deep familiarity with the work.'

When I became a film critic, I wondered if I could follow Cardus's example – take the plot from the synopsis always provided by the publicity people, then add director and stars in the first paragraph, then how the film was shot and performed in the last. 'Tomorrow, at the Odeon, Leicester Square, Mr George Lucas directs *Star Wars*, with Mr Harrison Ford, Ms Carrie Fisher and Mr Alec Guinness.' After the plot, previously given to the sub-editors, one could conclude, 'Mr Lucas marshals his special effects with spell-binding efficiency, and includes several comput-erised beasties in his cast. Mr Guinness shows Mr Ford and Ms Fisher how to act, but the beasties almost equal him. Expect a considerable success.' It would have made things so much easier.

It was something of a fluke that I progressed from correcting other people's copy and designing pages towards writing. The film job came my way largely, I suspect, because a new editor didn't know what to do with me and took a chance. But I have to say this. No film I ever saw was any more dramatic than the story of my parents, whose marriage was overtaken so soon by a tragedy that received huge publicity and effectively destroyed the happiness of both. That they remained together for the rest of their lives afterwards has always been a conundrum to me. I shall never wholly solve it and, by now, have given up trying.

The last thing I could predict was the trouble I fell into which, for a brief moment, looked as if what happened to Baumberg would happen to me. And for the same reason.

CHAPTER 12

FULL CIRCLE

By now I had been summoned by the *Guardian* to its offices in London, which were then in Grays Inn Road, and was ensconced as a sub-editor in the Features Department. I did occasional pieces for the arts pages but my main job was designing, editing copy and finally going down to make sure a compositor would put the hot metal into the correct hole. I enjoyed working with the compositors and they seemed to like me, especially when I became their bookmaker of choice, because I gave them better odds than Ladbroke's or William Hill. I'd let them bet on anything, Wimbledon included, and, because of this, I nearly came badly unstuck. In order to tempt them, I gave them odds of 1000–1 on horses, dogs, teams or sportsmen I felt sure were not going to win. One of those certain losers was Fred Stolle, the Australian tennis player. He was an expert in doubles but not in the first rank as a singles player. Accordingly, I offered odds of 1000–1 on him winning Wimbledon. Two compositors took up the challenge and had £1 on Fred. That meant I would lose £2000 if he won and I would be even more popular in the composing room. When he reached the quarter finals, I grew uneasy. When he got into the semis, I started to shake. And when he served and volleyed his way to the final, I was beside myself. The two compositors looked at me with unalloyed glee. I'd have to pay or I'd never get my pages done satisfactorily again.

To my great good fortune Fred lost; though he put up a splendid fight, which had me on the edge of my seat in front of the television, sweating profusely. I gathered up my measly £2 the next day with as straight a face as I could muster. 'Bad luck!' I said to the compositors as if I actually meant it.

'You lucky little sod!' one of them commented.

The next day I went to Heathrow Airport on my way to a much-needed holiday. And there, sitting disconsolately waiting for his plane to Australia, was Fred Stolle surrounded by his rackets. Taking my courage into my hands, I went up to him and commiserated. I also told him the story of my bet. To his credit, he laughed heartily. 'Glad somebody got some satisfaction out of it,' he said. 'But if I'd held my serve in the fourth set, I'd have won the fifth. You were a lucky man.' This taught me the one vital thing about betting. If someone gives you ridiculously long odds, always take them. You might just win. When I told my father, who liked a bet, he told me he was once offered 1000–1 on a horse running in the Grand

National by a course bookmaker. He didn't take it and the horse won. It was a no-hoper called Foinavon and the reason he won was a gigantic pile-up halfway through the race, which disposed of almost all the fancied horses. They either fell or had to be pulled up. Little Foinavon, once being a polo pony, skipped neatly over the fallen horses and the fence, and was several hundred yards ahead before the few remaining competitors were able to give chase. Even then, he was nearly beaten but was so far ahead that he managed, although almost at a walk, to win. Once again my father had made the wrong decision. But this time I had total sympathy with him.

Although a sub-editor at the *Guardian*, I was allowed to write for other publications provided they were magazines and not rival newspapers. I was given a rather odd commission by a then prominent weekly magazine. It was to go round the strip clubs of Soho, find out what was on offer, how much the show cost and interview some of the girls who worked in them. In particular, I was asked to find out about some of the private clubs in or near Mayfair which allegedly put on pornographic displays for their favoured clients, among whom, it was rumoured were a good many celebrities. There was said to be one club which specialised in such shows, starring a huge and well-endowed Nigerian called Superman. He would have sex on the stage with a very small Chinese woman to the 'ohs' and 'ahs' of the audience, and finally call for any female member of the audience to join in. I found where the club was but also that it cost £100 to enter – a considerable sum in the sixties. There were bouncers at the door on the lookout for either the police or the press. The magazine quibbled at the cost and wouldn't pay the £100. So I never got in but did manage to gather details from one client that there were several famous faces among the audience, and that some of the women did indeed join Superman and the Chinese girl on stage.

I wrote this all down as part of my 1500-word piece, but it was too hot for the magazine to handle. They preferred the stuff about the more orthodox strip clubs where some of the hostesses went off with the customers, some just did their strip act and moved on to the next club and some simply danced without much on. Customers had to pay an entrance fee of £10 to £20, and a similar figure for a drink for themselves and the hostess. If you got away with spending less than £100 during the evening, you were pretty lucky.

In the end, the article cost me considerably more than the magazine was prepared to pay, either in expenses or in fees, since I visited six or seven clubs and attempted to interview several of the women who worked there. The editor got cold feet and spiked the whole thing. The girls I thought were pretty nice, and not just physically. Very few of them supplemented their incomes with prostitution. The strippers and dancers worked hard until about 4 a.m. and then went home, often to husbands and live-in men friends. They didn't so much despise their customers as feel sorry for them. They considered them lonely or frustrated people, many of them tourists, spending a large amount of their hard-earned money on nothing very much. There were some acts on the often makeshift stages where sex was simulated but the eroticism on display was hardly more than cursory. The police, I assumed, saw to that.

One girl I met at a Soho club was particularly frank about her part-time occupation as a hostess. She was from a working-class home in the north of England, had left there for London at the age of sixteen and got herself hooked on morphine. Though she had now kicked the habit, she had drifted into club life through a contact, largely because it was better paid than the menial jobs she had previously done. She was married and had a child by a man whom she had now left. Apart from being attractive, she was a nice girl and certainly a brave one, having survived more in her short life than most of us have in a long one. And though we were totally different in every possible way, I began to make dates with her. I was living in a small one-bedroom flat in Highgate Village at the time and soon she was coming there to see me. It was an unlikely liaison but one I could not resist, even when she told me that the man she had married was looking for her and badly wanted her back, possibly because of the child he was now looking after.

What she didn't tell me until the affair was in full flow was that he had been, and possibly was still, connected to the notorious Kray Brothers. Before their incarceration, they ruled large areas of London and were wont now and then to throw those who crossed them off the top of the nearest tower block. This made me distinctly nervous and, to my chagrin, it wasn't long before her husband managed to contact her again. She told him that she wanted to keep seeing her child but not him. Not surprisingly, he wasn't satisfied. I finally realised that, however I played it, I could find myself in deep trouble. Working as I did from about 4 p.m. often until well after midnight, I grew more and more nervous about going home to Highgate at night, with or without the girl. So we often met outside the *Guardian* buildings, or near the club where, unbeknown to him, she worked. We would stay the night together in one or other of the many bed and breakfast establishments dotted around the King's Cross area. It seemed too dangerous to go home to Highgate. He was, she said, a man who could well be violent, and I had the suspicion that he knew someone else was involved and had an inkling that it was me.

It was the middle of summer and one of England's rare heatwaves had struck. I went to bed, fortunately alone, without pyjamas and no blanket or sheet to cover me. At 3.30 a.m. I awoke with a start. A man was standing beside the bed, bending over my naked body with some sort of implement in his hand. Without even looking, I knew exactly who it was. I thought that I was about to die, and it flashed through my mind straight away that my father had killed someone who was having an affair with my mother, and now the family history was going to repeat itself.

I don't know what made me then do what I did, except the realisation that it was no use countering any violence with any feeble attempts of my own. So I looked up from the bed and said, as calmly as I could, 'Hullo, Frank.' Whereupon Frank, who was indeed the husband of my girl-friend, started to hit me round the head with his cosh. When you are entirely naked and totally uncovered, and have just been awoken from sleep in the middle of the night, you feel as vulnerable as it is possible to be. So I rolled up in a kind of ball, almost into a foetal position, and tried to protect my head with my hands. I don't know how long he kept hitting me, but it can't have been very long. Then he suddenly stopped and said, 'Christ, I can't hit a man who doesn't hit back. Get up and make me a cup of coffee.' With blood streaming from my head and hands, I got up and, still stark naked, went from my bedroom into the kitchen while Frank made himself comfortable on the sitting-room sofa. I noticed that he was only a medium-sized, not very tough-looking man of around thirty-five, with a pasty face and slicked-back hair. He wasn't quite the thug I had expected from his police reputation. Nor did he seem, once he'd stopped hitting me, as angry as he had a right to be. It struck me that he was, at base, as vulnerable as I was. I wasn't in a fit state, however, to argue with him for too long. It was best, I thought, to be as calm as possible. Without any clothes on, though, it was difficult to be dignified.

When I came back with the coffee, he said, in a very matter-of-fact tone, 'You've been fucking my wife, haven't you?'

'No,' I said, 'she's just a friend.'

Looking me up and down, with an expression on his face that suggested I was something he ought to squash on the floor, he said, 'No, I don't suppose you have. You're queer, aren't you? You're a bloody faggot!'

It was the chance of a lifetime and I took it. 'Yes,' I said. 'I am.'

'Thought so,' he said. 'A proper man would have hit me back. But you know where my wife is, don't you?'

'No,' I said. 'I have no idea.'

I don't think he believed me, but he started to drink his coffee and warned me as he did so that if I ever associated with her again I would be 'dead meat'. He had friends who handled that sort of thing and he would send them after me. Finishing his coffee, he got up and said that he had got to go because he had a 'job' to do before it was light.

And with that, he calmly left the flat through the front door. To this day, I don't know how he got in, though the bedroom window was wide open because of the heat and he might have scaled the drainpipe.

I was in the bathroom wiping the blood off my head when I heard a knock on the front door. I thought it was the landlord, woken by the noise. But, gingerly opening the door, this time in my underpants, I saw it was Frank again. He brushed past me into the sitting room, and took off first a shoe and then a sock. Out of the sock he produced £40 of my money. Handing it to me, he said, 'And next time don't leave this lying about.' Then he left, without another word.

So history didn't repeat itself, but, after that experience, I was even more terrified that it might. The next day I went straight to Highgate Police. They were not very helpful – the view being that, if I was indeed 'messing about' with someone else's wife, I couldn't expect 'a clear run'. They did, however, look up Frank's record, which was extensive, and warned me to keep clear of him. 'He knew what he was doing giving you the money back,' the detective-sergeant said. 'Because if he hadn't we could have charged him with breaking and entering and burglary. But even then, he probably wouldn't have got much of a stretch in gaol and, when he came out . . .' I didn't let him finish the sentence. There was no offer of help. For the police, it was just another 'domestic'.

There didn't seem to be anyone to whom I could turn for advice. The obvious conclusion was that I should do what Frank said and leave the girl. But I could not. I continued to see her but not in my own flat. One day, by chance, I bumped into my father's old friend, the ex-heavyweight boxer, Don Cockell. I bought him a large one and told him my story. He was a good deal more sympathetic than the police. 'Well,' he said, 'if you're not going to leave the girl, I'll tell you what we'll do – I'll come up and stay at your place with you and, if Frank comes in again, I'll throw the bastard out of the window! You've got to meet like with like in this world.' It was an offer I found tempting, considering my state of mind – except for the fact that if Frank really did try to get into the flat again, I wasn't too happy about him being thrown out of the window. This could be construed as manslaughter rather than self-defence. I couldn't imagine explaining it away to Highgate Police. And maybe Frank's notorious friends would have something to say about it too and come after me.

In the end, I didn't take up Don's offer. But I did write a note to the editor of the *Guardian*, sealed it in an envelope and told his secretary not to open it or give it to him unless something untoward happened to me. In it, I put the name of the man who was after me, but not the reason why. Fortunately it was never opened and eventually I was able to take it back.

Not long afterwards, the detective-sergeant who had seen me at Highgate Police Station rang to tell me that Frank was in prison – he'd been apprehended attempting a burglary. It was, he said, laughing, a policeman's house and he'd got six months but would probably come out in four. 'Just thought you'd like to know,' the detective-sergeant said. 'It will give you a bit of a break. But he could come after you again.'

I did not take much comfort from this news. I still had visions, probably unfounded, of the psychotic Krays sending someone else round. But the next surprise call I got was from the Greek owner of the club where my girlfriend, now almost as scared as me but distinctly braver, still worked. He obviously considered me a hopeless case and he was right. He told me he was prepared to help me out. He said he liked my girlfriend, who was one of the few he employed who was never late for work, and he respected the fact that I was not prepared to desert her. 'But let's face it, you can't deal with this man and I can. It'll cost you a bit of money, but you won't hear from him again.'

'How much?' I heard myself asking. '£500,' he replied.

'But what would you do?' I enquired.

'It's easy,' he said. 'We'll find out the day he comes out and we'll send a car for him. We'll say Ronnie Kray wants to see him. That'll flatter him and he'll get in. He won't get out on his own two legs, I can tell you.'

I didn't really want to think about the implications of what he said. It was as if I were playing a part in a surreal black comedy. All I knew was that I wanted to be rid of Frank before he got rid of me, so I said, 'Cash or cheque?'

'Cash, please,' he said. 'You won't regret it,' adding that he was doing me a favour because I seemed like a decent man. I could give him the money now or when the job was done. I asked for a bit of time, wondering if I was dreaming the whole thing. But my head was still sore and I wasn't. Even so, I wasn't sure about the Greek. Perhaps he'd never do what he said and maybe I'd be relieved if he didn't. Confused as I was, I kept quiet. Only my girlfriend knew about the offer and she seemed perfectly happy about it. Frank wasn't Baumberg, but he was a lot more dangerous. I waited, and waited, dithering about whether to cancel the deal, but in the end went along with the plan. I paid the money in cash as the Greek had asked. My girlfriend and I continued our affair, now feeling better protected than by the police.

It is difficult not to smile at the memory of the whole business, and especially its ending, because it now seems so much like a fictional melodrama, even more so than my mother's fatal affair all those decades ago with its concomitant parts of horse-whips, duels, foreign villains and husbandly honour.

When the date passed for Frank to be released,

I got another phone call from the Greek. There had been a mistake with the date, he said, and Frank was not due out of gaol until the following week. Did I still want him to go ahead? This time I did not hesitate. I told him to forget the whole thing. I got the feeling he was as relieved as I was and he promptly returned the money. But he repeated that he was still perfectly prepared to go ahead with the original plan on the new date. I said no and ventured to enquire more precisely about Frank's fate had the plan remained. 'Don't ask or I might tell you,' is all he said.

I never saw or heard of Frank or the Greek again. My girlfriend and I eventually parted, and a friend of mine said to me sternly, 'Don't touch married women again. It's almost never worth it.' He was right. Would that Baumberg had taken that advice.

When I think about my parents now, as I often do, I still find it impossible to recognise, in the two people I knew, the young lieutenant and his beautiful wife who played out their few weeks of destructive notoriety on the stage of the Old Bailey. I remember them instead as rather sad old people who had lived together for a whole life-time after the case. 'We stayed together because of you,' my mother had once told me. I would have had a considerably happier early life if they had not. I can remember thinking, over and over again, that when I grew up and had children, things would be very different.

The smallest of details now seem to me to illustrate what the cost of life's misfortunes were to them – the way, for instance, my mother and my father used to talk to themselves in the bathroom when they thought no one was listening. Both of them used to repeat two words in the bath while swishing the water around them. My mother's were 'Endless frustration . . . endless frustration'. My father's were 'Oh, dear . . . oh, dear . . . oh, dear'. I never said anything to my mother about those two words. But, when my father was at Moor Hall Hotel, he used to bellow his 'Oh, dears' so loudly that I was constrained by the owner of the hotel to tell him about it. Shortly afterwards he wrote me a letter: 'My dear Derek – You'll be glad to know that the "oh, dears" are now under control. Strange. I was never aware I was saying them.'

I remember him now – and I persist in calling him my father whether he was or not – practising his golf swing again and again in the garden with gritted teeth that made his whole face wrinkle with concentration, and hissing through them, 'Left arm straight, bend at the knees, feet firm, wrists loose . . . Whack! . . . Follow through . . . oh, dear, oh, dear.' Or sitting in his favoured armchair (which I still have) smoking a pipe of his favourite Players Plain Tobacco, reading some military biography from colonial times, or even the book on André Gide I dared to give him one Christmas. 'I quite like old Gide,' he had later commented. 'Interesting old bugger. But of course he *was* a bugger.' There is also a treasured photograph of him standing proudly, puffing out his chest as if standing to attention beside me, with my three-year-old daughter in my arms, in the gardens of Moor Hall Hotel.

Douglas Malcolm with Derek and
his daughter Jackie at Moor Hall.

I remember my mother in her dressing gown, lying on the sitting-room sofa petting her favourite Persian cat, and now and then letting out a peal of laughter when one or other of us succeeded in mimicking a particular specimen of Bexhill-on-Sea's many odd characters – the pot, you might well say, calling the kettle black. Even my father would occasionally look up from his book and manage a laugh at times. I also remember the dreadful moment when she came rushing into my bedroom at 2 Channel View, with her nightdress ablaze after falling asleep to near the fire.

I try not to remember her last years when she scarcely knew who I was since, at her best, she had such remarkable warmth and a way of talking to you as if you were the only important person in the world. Sometimes, before she altered so sadly, I would go into her bedroom after breakfast and sit with her talking as she lay in her bed beginning the long and subtle task of making herself up for the day. 'If you put cream on your face,' she used to say, as if I might very well do so, 'always rub it gently upwards, never downwards. And don't use soap on it, my little man. It's terrible for one's complexion. Porridge is the very best thing, but your father keeps on eating the oats I buy.' She would then bring out the latest edition of *Prediction*, a popular magazine of the day, and look up our fortunes. She was Aquarius and I was Taurus. Nothing seemed terribly accurate to me. But she invariably found the truth between the lines and, when her mid-morning cup of tea was brought, she'd drink it, turn the cup upside down and examine the tea leaves for further enlightenment. Why she bothered I don't know, since Nostradamus, who seemed to be a regular contributor, invariably suggested that the world was in any case going to end in dire circumstances very soon. These were our moments together, slightly absurd but oddly comforting to me. Would that there had been more of them.

You don't forget your parents, however strange and remote your childhood seems when you grow older and the world has changed. You forgive them most things in the end and remember the best of them. But you never forgive yourself for failing them, as I felt I had, at least in my father's final days when he desperately wanted to come to live with me. And the strange thing is that, in the end, you become more and more like them, whether you intend to or not. You use the phrases they used and begin, now and then, to suspect they are watching you from somewhere up there in the ether. I like to think they are now pleased I am very happily married. And I hope, wherever they are, they'll forgive me telling their story. But it is, at least partly, mine too.